A Leader's Job
is To look into The
future And see The
organization, Not as iT i
but As iT should be.

7/ ?/
2/ 24/1?

ToHAH V A

Embrace the
IMPOSSIBLE

WANda Ngai
VA   7/2/09

Wonderful !!

Other books by William G. Johnsson:
Jesus: A Heart Full of Grace
Mark: The Gospel of Jesus

To order, call **1-800-765-6955**.

Visit us at
www.reviewandherald.com
for information on other Review and Herald® products.

WILLIAM G. JOHNSSON

Embrace the IMPOSSIBLE

It's the Story of the Bible.

It's the Story of the
Seventh-day Adventist Church.

And It's My Story.

This book was
Edited by Penny Estes Wheeler
Cover designed by Trent Truman
Cover art by Joel D. Springer
Interior design by Tina M. Ivany
Typeset: Bembo 12/15

PRINTED IN U.S.A.

13 12 11 10 09   1 2 3 4 5

Library of Congress Cataloging-in-Publication Data
Johnsson, William G., 1934- .
  Embrace the impossible: it's the story of the Bible. It's the story of the Seventh-day Adventist Church and it's my story / William G. Johnsson.
      p. cm.
1. Johnsson, William G., 1934- 2. Seventh-Day Adventists—Biography. I. Title.
  BX6193.J635A3 2008
  286.7092—dc22
  [B]
                                            2008031882
ISBN 978-0-8280-2355-9

To those intrepid men and women who
slogged and dreamed along with me
in the *Review* office 1982-2006:

Rachel (who typed this manuscript) and Roy,
Bill and Bonita
Carlos and Kimberly
Steve and Merle, Myron and Myrna
Ella, Aileen, and Andy, Jean and Jeanne
Jocey and Jim, Gene and George

Plus:
Chitra and Corinne
Jackie, Kit, and Debbie
Ruth, Mary, and Nicole

Viva la compagne!

Contents

Preface

One day as I approached the close of my long tenure as editor of the Adventist Review, I felt a strange sensation come over me. It was as though I had been away for 20 years and had come home.

It was a long journey. Not 20 years but 25, a quarter century of intense, focused, demanding but ultimately blessed service in the cockpit of the Seventh-day Adventist Church. My unique responsibilities made me a confidant of three General Conference presidents, to whom I reported directly. It put me on committees and commissions, made me both participant and chronicler of events that shaped the worldwide Adventist movement.

I was there when one of my bosses faced the most crushing blow of his long, distinguished career. I was there when another went through a huge personal crisis that threatened the church at large. I was there when the role of women in ministry was discussed and debated, when decisions were taken that left some members elated and others deflated. I was there when theological issues hung over the church, when administrative mistakes made many angry and disillusioned.

I was there. I saw, I heard, I wrote. And I spoke. I cast my vote.

But it was more than a quarter century of turbulence and sharp turns. It was a time of unprecedented progress and growth as the church I love morphed into a global community with increasing impact on society. For the Lord was *in* the church and *with* the church—of this I am 100 percent sure. Through the struggles and disappointments, through the threats and challenges, in the incredible expansion in numbers and in the growing corporate likeness into the image of Christ—God was there.

I have come home now. And before the scenes of those 25 years—years of privilege, years of hard work that taxed me to the limits of my personal reserves and beyond, but years of deep satisfaction and fulfillment—begin to fade, it's time to share them with the church. I believe strongly that the church is for all, not just for those in leadership. I believe in the right of all members to know what is happening without distortion or evasion. So I will tell the story of those 25 years as I saw it.

However, don't look for a "kiss and tell" book, an exposé. I have low regard for those individuals who, granted access to the inner circles of an organization, sell their soul for fame or filthy lucre. Some matters, some details, will remain with me, as they should. And while I hope and pray that this memoir will be honest and candid, I also want it to be fair and kind. The Lord knows I have plenty of flaws myself. There's no need to try to mask them by pointing up the foibles and failings of those with whom I worked closely.

In several places in the book I employ direct speech in recounting conversations. I have reconstructed these. My account is true to the ideas conveyed, although the actual words may have been different.

This memoir focuses on my quarter-century at church headquarters. It was, I believe, a time that Adventists, more and more, began to embrace the impossible; that dreams turned into reality before their eyes and they saw the working of the Lord who calls into life new things out of nothing.

The story of this book is wider, however. It is also my story, and so, while it is not a full-blown autobiography, it shares how I came to be placed in such a position of high trust and responsibility, and how the story goes on even after I came home.

For my God-blessed life as well as for the church, the story is all about embracing the impossible.

The Impossible

CHAPTER 1

The Boy in the Biggin

With man this is impossible, but with God all things are possible.
—Jesus Christ (Matthew 19:26)

On October 27, 1728, a boy was born in Marton in Yorkshire, England. He would grow up to rewrite the map of the world.

Nothing could have seemed less likely at the boy's birth. He was born in a mud-and-thatch hovel known in those parts as a *biggin*. It had but two small rooms with a dirt floor, and farm animals wandered in and out.

Life expectancy was low. Four siblings perished before the age of 5: Mary, Mary (pathetically named for the deceased sister, but also doomed to die young), Jane, and William. An older brother, John, died at age 23.

The boy's father worked as a day laborer, making the prospects bleak indeed for his surviving son. The boy would not go to school. In fact, public education did not exist. His would be a life of hardscrabble poverty, always focused on earning enough to put bread on the table. He could not expect to travel or to improve his lot in life. His would be like those of generations before him—narrow, confined, chained by circumstances beyond his making or control.

A day's walk in radius—this would be the extent of his journeys. Like his father, he would follow the well-trod loop between home, field, and church. And when the end came, he would join his parents and siblings in the crowded family grave plot in the churchyard.

That this boy would burst the chains of family and upbringing and become one of the greatest adventurers the world has seen—

who could have predicted it? That his three epic voyages into realms unknown—into the one third of the earth's surface that lay unexplored; home, it was said, to strange sea creatures and fabulous new lands—would open the world to the modern era of travel, who would be so bold as to give words to the idea?

Impossible.

Yet the boy in the biggin would sail 200,000 miles in small wooden ships—as far as the moon is from earth. He would sail farther and farther south, seeking the fabled continent of *terra australis* that from ancient times had been speculated to exist as a balancing weight to the land mass of Europe. Onward and farther would he press, until he had crossed 70 degrees of latitude and, only 70 miles from Antarctica, endured cold that turned the ship's sails to sheets of lead and the ropes to iron cables. Then, having exploded the myth of the great south continent, he would turn north, sailing further and still further in search of a passage across the top of the world. Ever onward he would journey, into cold and mist and treacherous Alaskan waters that even today test the courage of ships' captains and the mettle of their navigational instruments, until he had crossed 70 degrees north.

Could this child, born without hope or prospect of education, pen a million words in his ships' journal during the seven years of his incredible voyages?

Impossible.

Could he acquire such mathematical skills that the charts he mapped of new lands were so accurate that they still would be used two centuries after his death?

Utterly impossible.

Could the boy in the biggin, born and raised on the lowest rung of England's social ladder, who married a woman likewise of low standing—daughter of a dockside tavern keeper—rise to membership in the Royal Society, reserved for the country's intellectual elite?

Nonsense. Only in dreams and novels can fantasies like these be given a hearing.

Yet James Cook, explorer extraordinaire, made the dreams come true, turned fiction into reality in the story of his life, which is every bit as extraordinary as the story of his voyages.

Reaching the 71st degree south of latitude, in the grip of howling Antarctic gales, Cook wrote in his journal: "Ambition leads me not only farther than any other man has gone before me, but as far as I think it possible for man to go."★

James Cook embraced the impossible.

Cook did not die in his native land; his body did not join the crowded family plot in the Marton churchyard. His end came in place and manner about as far from the sodden Yorkshire biggin as geography allows or the imagination can stretch. James Cook was speared and clubbed to death by natives of the Hawaiian islands.

Which he discovered.

———◦◆◦———

Long before James Cook was born in the Yorkshire biggin another bold adventurer wrote, "It has always been my ambition to preach the gospel where Christ was not known, so that I would not be building on someone else's foundation" (Rom. 15:20). The apostle Paul, explorer extraordinaire for the Lord Jesus Christ, embraced the impossible.

The original apostles, all of whom were Jews, focused their missionary efforts on fellow Jews or Gentiles who had been attracted to Judaism. But the risen Lord had commanded that the good news should go to the whole world (Matt. 28:18-20; Acts 1:8), and He chose the unlikeliest person to initiate the global mission. Putting His hand on Saul of Tarsus, strict Pharisee and persecutor of Christians, the Lord commissioned him: "Go; I will send you far away to the Gentiles" (Acts 22:21).

From a human perspective, the task given Paul was impossible. How could the Roman Empire, proud of its might and civilization, satisfied with its pantheon of gods, be led to embrace a new religion? And *such* a new religion! No heroic figure here, no clever teacher, but a crucified carpenter, whom His followers alleged to have risen from the dead.

The new faith had no legal standing. It attracted, not the wise and the powerful, but the poor and the lowly, slaves and servants. "Not many of you were wise by human standards; not many were influential; not many were of noble birth. But God chose the foolish things of the world to shame the wise; God chose the weak things of the world to shame the strong," Paul wrote to the believers in Corinth (1 Cor. 1: 26, 27).

And the impossible became reality. Points of light began to glow in city after city; in synagogues and homes; and, at last, even in Caesar's own palace.

The message of the crucified Carpenter who rose from the dead was unstoppable.

God loves the word *impossible*. "Is anything too hard for the Lord?" we read in the Old Testament (Gen. 18:14). And in the New, Jesus says, "What is impossible with men is possible with God" (Luke 18:27), and "Everything is possible for him who believes" (Mark 9:23).

The Bible is a book of heroes. Ordinary people do extraordinary things as they trust God and He empowers them.

Moses, raised in Pharaoh's palace, turns his back on Egyptian royalty and leads a slave rabble to freedom.

David, still a young man wet behind the ears, takes on a giant with five smooth stones and a slingshot.

Esther, beautiful queen of the Persians, puts her crown and her life on the line to help rescue the people of her birth.

Daniel, revered elder statesman, prays undaunted with window open and emerges unscathed from the den of lions.

Before ordinary men and women barriers fail and fortresses crumble. The weak become strong; faintedhearted act like heroes. They perform amazing feats—feats undreamed of—because, touched by God, they embrace the impossible.

And why? Because, before they ever attempted the impossible, they laid hold on the Power that motivated the apostle Paul. This is an idea so way out, so far beyond the range of human experience, that most others never entertain it. This is the certainty that God *is* and that He can be known personally, that He is infinite in love and goodness, that He loves us with a passion stronger than death, and that—in spite of our unworthiness—He regards us as His sons and daughters.

This is grace.

To live in grace is to embrace the impossible.

More and more, I love the word *impossible*. I don't want to flee from it, don't want to dismiss it. I want to live in it. I want to embrace it.

Embracing the impossible. It's the story of the Bible. It's the story of the Seventh-day Adventist Church. And it's my story.

---

*Quoted in Tony Horwitz, *Blue Latitudes: Boldly Going Where Captain Cook Has Gone Before* (New York: Picador), p. 210. I am indebted to Tony Horwitz for the facts about Captain Cook used in this chapter.

The Road to Washington

CHAPTER 2

Follow the Gleam

After it, follow it,
Follow the Gleam.
—Alfred Lord Tennyson

M y experience with the impossible began, perhaps, in a little Adventist church in the city of Adelaide in southern Australia. I was a shy, gangly 15-year-old who loved books and studies—a "swot" in the vernacular of the day. But at the time, my life was in more than the usual teenage transition.

Saturday mornings my dad would put on his suit and tie and be off to catch the trolley into the city. He was always early for Sabbath school, where he taught a class in the front left side of the Seventh-day Adventist church at 82 Angas Street. Joel Johnsson was a fixture among the saints. Never late, unvarying in habits and rectitude.

Dad went off carrying his Bible, while I caught the trolley carrying a bag with my cleated boots and football uniform. I played on the high school football team—football being of the Australian rules variety, that unique blend of long kicking, leaping catches, and nonstop action with 18 players per side on a grass "oval" 180 yards long.

I loved studies, and I loved football. But at 15 I dropped off the team and began to observe the Sabbath. I was the youngest of nine children, and none of my siblings kept the Sabbath, nor did my mother.

At first I observed the Sabbath privately, staying at home and reading. But then, encouraged by Dad, I began to attend the young people's meetings on Saturday afternoon in the little church on Angas Street. I would slip in quietly, sit on the back pew, and be out the door like a rocket as soon as the meeting closed.

One Sabbath afternoon as I sat on the back row I was suddenly confronted by the impossible. The leader of the meeting came to me and asked me to assist in collecting the offering. I shrank at the prospect and wanted to refuse, but somehow I found grace to say yes. I went through the motions, getting the dreaded task over with as soon as possible, and returned to the back row, wondering if I would ever come back to this place of horrors.

But I did, again and again. When the summer came and the Adventists pitched tents for their annual camp meeting, I went along with Dad. And when on Sabbath morning the preacher from America invited those who had never accepted Jesus as Savior and Lord to stand up and walk to the front of the big tent, I was one of those who responded.

Now Dad had someone to accompany him to church each Saturday morning. Together he and I would be off to the trolley and the city, where I would sit in his Sabbath school class, while back at home my mother and siblings observed with displeasure the changes taking place in my life and practices.

After some time in the little church—maybe when I was 17—the impossible reared its head again. Someone got the crazy idea that I should teach a class in the Sabbath school. Even more crazy, I accepted the invitation. My friend of long standing, Ron Burns, remembers the morning I stood in front of the class for the first time. My hands shook visibly, and my knees knocked!

Who could have dreamed that someday I would address audiences around the world, from small groups to those numbering in the many thousands; that I would speak with television cameras rolling or to thousands of unseen radio listeners in wide-flung places?

I certainly did not. A thought like that seemed impossible. It was beyond me. I did not aspire to it. In fact, I was scared of it.

The good Lord leads us one step at a time. He does not show us a future that would overwhelm us. He merely asks us to say yes to the step that lies immediately before us. Where that step, and the next, and the next may ultimately take us is up to Him.

When we look back, the impossible may seem altogether ordinary. What is impossible about helping to collect the offering in a little church? What is terrifying about leading a class of a dozen or so people in a study of the Word? After you have taught hundreds of classes and preached thousands of sermons, as I have, the impossible shrinks in size.

So the impossible seems impossible because of the voices in our heads. When we turn the impossible over to God, He makes it look easy.

God loves that word *impossible*.

So do I. More and more I want to embrace it.

My mother was a small woman who was large in good works. As I remember her in her final years, a frail old woman approaching 90, she stood barely five feet tall. She probably had lost several inches from her youth, but I doubt that at any time in her life she weighed more than 110 pounds.

Yet this little Australian woman gave birth to nine children. She married a tall, husky, hazel-eyed Swedish sailor who settled down in South Australia and later became a Seventh-day Adventist.

I was the youngest of the nine. Perhaps because I was her "baby," perhaps because I came along after she thought her child-bearing years were over (she used to refer to me as "something of a miracle"), I had a sense of special love. Of all the brood, I became the most attached to home and family.

Yet, as life would turn out, I would be the only one to leave home. To this day all of my brothers and sisters still live in Australia, most within easy access of our old family home.

Although Noelene and I, and our children, regularly came back to Australia to see her—first from India, later from the United States—

during the last 22 years of my mother's life not once were we present for a Mother's Day or a Christmas. Our children, born in India, were ages 4 and 2 before she saw them. And that separation, I think, has been the most difficult part of our service for the Lord.

Yet never did I hear her complain. Until her final years she wrote faithfully, at least every week, and her letters and occasional phone calls left us in no doubt about how she longed to see us. But in spite of her great love—perhaps because of it—she was able to let me and her other children go. As much as she hated the leaving, she knew that each of us must march to the beat of our own drummer.

That is one of her great influences upon me—the sense of her accepting, forgiving love that did not attempt to dictate my life.

Another is her great moral strength. She had deep blue eyes and a firmly set jaw. She read widely, formed her opinions, and wasn't afraid to express them. Ours was a home marked by lively discussion and debate, argument and exchange of ideas.

And she was a woman rich in good works—that is my final memory of her. All during any given year she was planning birthday parties, preparing gifts, and organizing the Big Event—the annual Johnsson Christmas party. With children and spouses, grandchildren and great-grandchildren, plus other relatives and friends who were always made welcome, these were gala occasions. She always had a gift for each one who came, generally made with her own hands.

But her kindness went further. She invited shut-ins home for a Christmas meal, hiring a taxi to bring them from an old people's home so they could sit down and enjoy Christmas at our table. If Christianity is shown by kindness and loving hospitality to the fortunate and the unfortunate, my mother embodied it.

As I look back on my life, I now realize that I had the great good fortune to grow up in an environment in which I never doubted that I was loved. It was a warm, safe environment; an environment of hard work and good food and fun always within the confines of the family.

What tribute can I bring to the memory of this small blue-eyed

Aussie who gave me life and set me on the right path? What would please her most, I think, would be flowers. She loved her garden and spent much time in it, especially after her children were grown and gone. Our house wasn't the grandest on the street, but it always had the prettiest garden.

And so, in honor of my mother, a bouquet of roses!

When I was 10 or 11 my father gave me a wonderful gift. It was a gift that changed me and has stayed with me to this day.

Dad encouraged me to read the Bible. He followed the practice of reading through the Bible every year, and he invited me to do likewise.

My earliest memory of Dad is the same as the last memories: up early in the morning, alone, reading the Bible. He always started the day with a cold shower and the Scriptures. I didn't take to the first practice, but the second one stuck.

My dad had little formal education. Born in Stockholm, Sweden, of Lutheran parents, he went to sea at age 14. He sailed the world on sailing vessels, spending months away, weathering the storms of Cape Horn before the Panama Canal was completed. Years later we all sat enthralled as he told and retold stories of life before the mast—adventures, good times and bad times, including months of hunger at the hands of a cruel captain and an unscrupulous ship's purser.

On one of his voyages Dad's ship sailed down to Australia and anchored at Port Adelaide. While he was there, one night a group of young people—a glee club from St. Andrews church—gave a program at the sailors' mission. Through that seemingly chance encounter Joel Johnsson, a tall strapping Swede who knew no English except cusswords, met Edith Painter, a petite, pretty, feisty brunette.

Dad sailed back to Sweden, completed his contract, and then returned to Australia as an immigrant to seek out the young woman who had won his heart. Edith shocked her family—staunch Anglicans all, pillars of St. Andrews—by breaking her engagement to the young man approved by the Painters, and marrying the sailor with no prospects.

As I think back on my father, gone now for more than 40 years, I find it hard to imagine what he was like when Edith first met him. I remember him as a kind, gentle, godly man that one would never imagine to have lived the harsh, rough life of a sailor in those times.

After his conversion Dad's life changed, changed radically. "To all who received him [that is, Jesus], to those who believed in his name, he gave the right to become children of God—children born not of natural descent, nor of human decision or a husband's will, but born of God" (John 1:12, 13).

At some point Joel Johnsson opened his heart to Jesus. He "received him." He believed in His name. And he became a new person, a different person, a better person. It was as though he had been born again—born of God.

I wish I knew when and how Dad was led to accept Jesus. So many questions I have now that only he could answer, questions I never thought to ask him. Such is the way of a child with their parents. The child thinks the parents will always be there, but then the child leaves home, and before he knows it, the parents are gone.

This I do know, however: after Joel and Edith had been married for several years, he joined the Seventh-day Adventist Church. This is how it happened. The city of Adelaide, in the tradition of London's Hyde Park, set aside a public area where on Sunday afternoon anyone who wished could mount a soapbox and solve the problems of the world. One Sunday Dad went to the park and heard an Adventist preacher, E. B. Rudge. The speaker's remarks piqued his interest. Before long he was getting Bible studies, and at length he was baptized.

Edith also took Bible studies. The preacher who visited her, however—so she recounted the story much later—seemed heedless of the crying babies and of her pressing household tasks. Edith, whose religion was strongly practical, was turned off by his behavior. Whatever the truth of his doctrines, the preacher didn't act like a Christian in her book. She stayed with the Anglican Church.

The Adventist message took deep root in Joel's life. He became unswervingly upright in character. Years later, when as a ministerial student I preached in Adventist churches around Adelaide, I met people who volunteered: "Your father was the hardest worker in the building industry"; "Your father is the most honest man in this town."

Sometime—I don't know when—Dad began to get up early to read the Bible. He became thoroughly versed in it, not as a scholar, but as one who loved his Lord devoutly and came to the Word as his daily bread. He served on the conference committee, preached occasionally, helped start a new congregation, and is still most remembered for the Sabbath school class he taught until a few months before his death at age 80.

Raising a large family in those difficult years must have been very hard for Edith and Joel. I was born smack-dab in the heart of the Depression—in 1934. Another mouth to feed and another body to clothe surely meant that my coming into the world brought mixed feelings. Yet as I look back it seems that I was bathed in unconditional love.

My oldest siblings recall the good times before the Depression hit—pretty dresses and birthday parties with lots of presents. Dad worked in the building trade and earned good money. The Johnsson family had the means to send their children to church school.

Then the economic ceiling caved in around the world. Building activity stopped first, as it always does in a downturn. Dad found himself in the same condition as thousands of other men who wanted to work—laid off. It was desperate straits for the father of a large family.

Dad never went on government relief—the dole, as it was disparagingly dubbed. He came up with an idea to bring in some income. He would start a little house-to-house business, taking items of clothing and toiletries to the farmers who grew apples, pears, peaches, and cherries in the hills above Adelaide. He would buy a horse and cart and make his way into the back roads and lanes of the hills where people lived quiet and isolated lives.

And he did. I have no recollection of the horse and cart, but I grew up with talk of the business still fresh in the family lore. Dad would be gone for long stretches, but when he came home he would bring supplies of fruit and vegetables and a little cash. Meanwhile Edith marshaled the children in utilizing the large lot on which the family home stood. She grew a garden, kept a cow, and harvested olives for sale.

Many years later I discovered a piece of the puzzle from those hard times. How did Dad, with money so tight, ever find the means to purchase the horse and cart for his little business?

Long after Dad had gone to his rest I found the answer. Home on furlough from India, I preached at the Adventist church in Busselton, Western Australia. After the service a man met me and began to talk about Dad. This is the story he told me.

Dad had a plan, but he had no money. He went to the church conference office and asked if they could help. "I'm sorry, Brother Johnsson," said the treasurer, "but we have no funds for your business."

Desperate, Dad walked the streets of Adelaide. He came upon the Methodist City Mission and on an impulse went in.

"Sir, I have this plan," he told the superintendent of the mission. "I have a large family to feed and if only . . . "

"How much do you need?"

"Fifty pounds." Dad must have choked at the words. That sounded like a huge amount in those tough times.

Without a word the superintendent went into another room. He came back with £50 that he handed to Dad.

And so the dark years passed and the family survived intact. My brothers all left school at age 14, the earliest the law allowed, to seek work to help the family out. I was the only one of the nine to have the opportunity to finish high school. In spite of the limited education, however, my siblings made their mark in the world. One brother, Doug, became a highly successful businessman and was honored by the national government with the Order of Australia. A sister, Gwen, has authored books and articles, written plays, and currently—in her 80s!—is working on a movie. Three others owned their own businesses.

We grew up poor, but I never felt poor. We knew hard work and pulling together as a family; we knew pride in the Johnsson name and sticking up for each other; we knew love.

The oldest child, Gladys, who was known from infancy as Bonnie, married first. I was named after her fiancé, Bill. (Later, another sister married a Bill, so there were three of us who answered to "Bill" at family gatherings.) After Bonnie married, several years went by before anyone else walked down the aisle, then we had a rash of weddings. So for years almost the entire family was intact, and that's how I remember it.

Ten of us around the long kitchen table that filled the room. Dad at one end, Mother at the other, and the rest of us in our places. Mother up and down, over to the stove and back again, bringing food, caring for our needs. Simple food, but tasty—and always with a home-cooked dessert.

And everybody talking, talking, talking. News, politics, sports. Difficult to get a word in. However, one subject was rarely discussed—religion. Long before I showed up, the wars of religion had been fought through, and an unspoken truce declared.

My father had a good mind. He loved to put teasers to us around the family, riddles about numbers or relationships. We would argue back and forth as to the correct answer. One perennial favorite that never failed to generate a lively exchange went like this:

A man is looking at a picture of a man. He says: "Sisters and brothers I have none. But this man's father is my father's son."

Who is the man in the picture?

Some siblings were emphatic that the picture was of the man himself. The correct answer, of course, is his son.

Dad would set us off and sit back and enjoy the argument. He loved to tell jokes, but he was a lousy storyteller. He would get so wrapped up in the humor that he could never get the punch line out cleanly. He would shake with laughter, tears rolling down his checks, as he choked on the punch line.

"What did you say?" we'd all cry out, although we had heard the joke before.

Dad would try to give the punch line again, and Mother would be saying, "Jack, stop it." (For some reason she called him Jack.)

That was my life as a child. A little radio. No TV. Instead, family games—Monopoly a favorite—work and play. Not a bad way to start life, I reckon.

Growing up, I wasn't a Christian, and I didn't read the Bible. But around age 10 or 11, encouraged by Dad, I began to read it—to read it all the way through. In the King James Version, of course.

Whenever I had a question, I would ask Dad about it. Sometimes he didn't have the answer, but would get the answer from a pastor. I remember coming across the word "Selah" in Psalms and asking Dad what it meant. He didn't know, but he found out for me.

There is power in the Bible. It is an old, old book—in fact, a library of 66 books—but a Life force throbs through it. It is God's Word to us, and if we permit it, that life will quicken and change us. "For you have been born again, not of perishable seed, but of imperishable, through the living and enduring word of God," Peter tells us (1 Peter 1:23).

I read the Bible through. I did it again. And again. And again. Inevitably I became a believer. And at age 16 I gave my heart to Jesus, was baptized, and joined the Seventh-day Adventist Church.

For almost as long as I can remember, I have read the Bible through every year. Don't ask me how many times. I don't keep count. The number of times isn't important; feeding on the Word is.

The New Testament is my field of academic discipline. For many years now my devotional practice entails starting the day with the Bible—as my father did. I begin each year with the New Testament and read it through in the original Greek. This takes me through March. For the next six months I read the Old Testament, Genesis to Malachi, in English (my Hebrew has rusted out!). Then I close out the year by working through the New Testament again in Greek.

My father left the smallest of legacies. In financial terms it was almost nothing.

But with his sweet partner, Edith, he left a treasure. The Johnsson Nine, men and women of moral character, have made society a safer and better place. Who can put a dollar tag on such an inheritance?

And my father left me a priceless gift. The practice of reading the Bible has molded and shaped me, indubitably for the better. The Word has become my daily bread, my comfort, my guide, my strength, my counselor, my hope. Through that Word I have come to know and to love the living Word, the Word made flesh, my Savior and Lord Jesus Christ.

And out of this dynamic a Gleam shined into the heart of a shy young man, the *swot*. A Gleam of a future far bigger and wider than the confines of home. A Gleam of something not seen or imagined, only felt as a tremble, a shiver within the soul.

A Gleam of the impossible.

CHAPTER 3

The Road Less Traveled

Two roads diverged in a wood, and I—
I took the one less traveled by,
And that has made all the difference.
—Robert Frost, "The Road Not Taken"

At age 16, accepting Jesus Christ as my Savior and Lord, I was baptized by immersion and joined the Seventh-day Adventist Church. That was the first and most critical step in a series of decisions that would take me along the road less traveled.

With increasing consternation the family had observed the changes occurring in my life—the interest in the Bible and in copies of *Signs of the Times*, the *Australasian Record*, *Steps to Christ*, *The Desire of Ages*, and other Adventist books and magazines that Dad left around the house. An avid reader, I was reading myself into Adventism.

One evening my brother Gordon invited me to go for a ride on his motorcycle. We sped over the miles, the wind licking our faces, and then stopped to buy milk shakes. As we sat drinking them, he said, "I've been noticing a change in you. You seem to be getting pretty interested in going to church with Dad. That's all right. But don't do anything yet—wait until you're at least 18. Then you'll know if you really want to be a Seventh-day Adventist."

He was too late. One Sabbath morning at camp meeting, I had gone forward in response to the preacher's call, and had joined the baptismal class. A big evangelistic campaign conducted by George Burnside was running in the Adelaide town hall. Like others in those times, the meetings went on for several months. Midway through the series the preacher set up a tank on the stage and spoke about baptism. I was one of those who went down into the water that night.

I had heard the call of Jesus. He had spoken to my heart, and I said yes. When He calls, the time is now, not a year or years hence, whatever others may urge.

I have never regretted that initial yes. All that I am I owe to Jesus and the Seventh-day Adventist Church. It is not a perfect church, for it is made up of flawed human beings like me, but it has a perfect Lord.

The hardest part was in relating to my mother. I was her youngest, and she looked upon me as something of a miracle child. We were very close. In choosing Adventism—in those days considered by many Australians as a religion on the margins of respectability, in contrast to the majority Anglican faith—was I, in some sense, repudiating what she stood for?

But Mother and I grew closer as a result of my choice. We both learned that in choosing Adventism, I did not and would not love her less. "Don't let religion become an obsession," she urged me several times, perhaps reflecting her view of Dad's single-minded devotion to the Lord and the Seventh-day Adventist Church, but she grew reconciled to the changes in my life.

I should add a footnote, even though it doesn't directly relate to the theme of this book. Many years later my oldest sibling, Bonnie, told Noelene and me that she had come very close to being baptized when she was 15. The date was set, and Bonnie was one of the candidates. But at the last moment something intervened, and she wasn't baptized.

However, Bonnie continued to think of herself as Adventist. Late in life—her husband Bill, having gone to his rest—she told us, "I could never join any church other than the Seventh-day Adventist." And so, in God's good time, she did. Sixty years after her nonbaptism she became a member of the church.

Bonnie's story is amazing and wonderful. I share it here because it makes my spirit sing and can bring a ray of hope to readers whose hearts grieve over dear ones who were raised in an Adventist environment but who turned away from this church.

———————◆———————

Studies came easy to me, and I was able to move through them at a fast clip. I breezed through the public high school—one that specialized in science and math rather than the humanities—and at age 15 passed the public examinations required for matriculation. Because 16 was the minimum age for university study, the school offered a year of advanced courses that, if completed successfully, could carry university credit.

Thus I commenced tertiary education with first-year math, chemistry, and physics already under my belt. In those heady days my friends and I all regarded science and its technology as king, and looked down our noses at students enrolled in liberal arts courses. I had decided on a career in industrial chemistry, and at age 19 I graduated with a degree in chemical technology.

And again faced decisions.

I qualified for the gold medal awarded to the student with the best grades, but there was a problem—the public ceremony fell on a Friday night. I passed up the evening and picked up the award privately the following week.

Then there was the question of what to do with the training I had completed. The head of the department, Professor Spooner, invited me to stay on and do further studies, picking up some teaching and working as his assistant.

But I said no. Conscious of the fact that I was the only child in the family to have had the opportunity to complete high school, I wanted to find employment and bring in income to help my parents, who by now were in their 60s. The technical high school I had attended was a public institution so it was free, but the school uniform, books, and equipment were not. My mother had worked cleaning the public school close to our home to help pay my expenses. The university studies had been easier, since I was awarded a scholarship that covered all expenses and provided a small living allowance. Now, with my studies behind me, I was itching to earn a salary and give back to my parents who had sacrificed much to help me get an education.

When I turned down Professor Spooner's offer, he had another suggestion. "I want you to work for someone who will advance your career," he told me, "and the chief chemist at the gas company is one of the best people I know to do that. They have an opening, and I will recommend you for the position."

I knew the gas company, not from experience but from the huge round storage tank with the expandable top that dominated the landscape at Port Adelaide where I went fishing. Many people used gas for cooking and heating; the gas was generated from coal, since natural gas had not yet been discovered in Australia.

The interview at the gas company was a breeze. Without the chief chemist's actual telling me so, I knew I had the job. However, I needed to make one matter clear. So just before leaving, I said to him, "Sir, I need to explain something to you. I am a Seventh-day Adventist and will not be able to work on Saturdays. That is when I go to church."

A change came over his face. "Sometimes we will need your assistance on Saturday mornings. Will you be able to work occasionally or in emergencies?"

"No, sir, I will not be able to work on Saturday, which is the Sabbath."

The interview closed, and I rode home on my motorcycle. As the miles passed I rehearsed the interview and had the strong feeling that the position that had been within my grasp had slipped away. And it had, as a letter that arrived a few days later confirmed. The letter stated that because of my inability to work Saturdays as needed, I would not be hired.

At the time I was disappointed. From this vantage point, however, the loss seems minimal. No loss at all when I consider how my life developed—the adventure, the travels, the personal growth. Comparing all that with the position at the gas works, I ultimately gained far more out of what I lost.

I think that is always true of the Lord's dealings with us. Following Him leads to something better, never worse.

That was true for me, even in the short run. I quickly found a job in the lab of a company specializing in surface coatings—paints, finishes for automobiles, refrigerators, washing machines, and so on. It was a large company with connections to Du Pont, and the lab kept busy a full contingent of industrial chemists testing and developing new products. I spent a couple happy years there and enjoyed the work. One of the last projects I worked on was exploring the industrial applications of a new line of resins that had just been developed—epoxies, known by the trade name Epikote.

***

The scene is still vivid in memory—an army parade ground with 800 soldiers drilling before the commanding officer. We have been in camp for several weeks; the Korean War is raging. All young men are conscripted into national service—the Australian equivalent of the draft—when they turn 18. We go through 98 days of training, followed by shorter stretches over the following three years.

The commanding officer looks over the parade and notices that one soldier does not carry a weapon. He calls over a junior officer and orders him to get the soldier off the parade ground.

I am that soldier. I am commanded to fall out and return to the barracks.

When I became a Christian and embraced the teachings of the Seventh-day Adventist Church, I accepted also the church's position of non-combatancy in times of war. The Australian government made a provision for "conscientious objectors," but it wasn't easy or automatic. You had to appear before a magistrate and face a cross-examination by a state's attorney. No one could speak on your behalf. You had to face the music alone. I was peppered with questions, including my understanding of Psalm 18:34, "He teacheth my hands to war" (KJV). But I stood my ground, and the magistrate granted my request to be exempted from bearing arms during the national service training.

As I look back on that scene of the parade ground, I find it extraordinary how the Lord empowered me to be the only soldier drilling without a rifle. The platoon leader, Sergeant Gloyne, badgered and threatened me, but I never did take up a weapon. You need to remember that all this took place while I was a shy, bookish teenager who was just finding his feet in the Seventh-day Adventist Church.

The Sabbath brought another test in the army camp. We had no leave for the first five or six weeks, and training went on six days per week, with church parade on Sunday. As the first Sabbath drew near I made a request to have Sabbaths off. The request went up the line all the way to the commanding officer, who ordered me to appear before him. I explained why I did not want to take part in the regular exercises on Sabbath, and he granted me the request.

So on Sabbaths, while the other soldiers went to their training, I took my Bible and went into the woods. Sundays they lined up and went to church; I worked.

I did not fit with the program of the camp. Eventually I was excused from training with the other soldiers in my platoon and assigned to other duties—first, in the camp hospital; later, in the officers' mess.

Those 98 days were hard, but they put the iron in my soul. Hating to stand alone, I learned to stand alone. The Lord stood by me, supplying grace all-sufficient for every situation. I was slowly learning to trust Him and to follow Him, come what may.

The remaining three years of training proved to be easy by comparison. We had to show up for drills one night per week. There were weekend bivouacs and an annual camp of about 10 days. But at these events there were other Adventist young men who also had taken a noncombatant stance, and by now the officers were acquainted with Adventist beliefs so excused us from training during Sabbath hours and gave us leave to attend church services.

By the end of the required national service I had earned a couple of stripes. The sergeant invited me to stay with the program, but I thanked him and declined. My military days were over.

———◆———

By now all my friends came from the church, which was occupying an increasing role in my life. I was elected to church office, then leader of the Young People's Society, which met Sabbath afternoons. More and more people—including older ones—began to come to the meetings. Then we expanded our outreach to minister to the needs of young people in isolated churches: carloads of us would drive out into the country, put on an afternoon program and run a social gathering Saturday night. Back in Adelaide we got together for a round of activities each Sunday that took the entire day—tennis, golf, hiking, and swimming.

But something else was also happening. I had forgotten all about it until recently when a friend, interviewing me, probed this period of my life in detail.

I had a girlfriend. Her name, shall we say, was Harriet.

Harriet and her family had joined the church in the same big-city evangelistic series during which I was baptized. After several years we began to date. Apparently we seemed well suited to each other, for our friends and the conference youth leader began to assume that we were on a track that would take us down the aisle.

I turned 21, an important milestone in Australian society at that time. Now I was legally an adult and could vote in elections (voting was, and still is, compulsory in Australia). My family gave me the traditional party and presented me, as was customary, with a large key signifying the key to the door—ironic, since our home was never locked, even when we went on vacation.

That night, the night of my twenty-first birthday, my friends expected that Harriet and I would announce our engagement. Although she never mentioned it, I am sure she was also anticipating it. After the party I drove her home, and we sat and talked. The air was heavy with expectancy, with the question hanging in the air, waiting for me to give it voice.

It seemed so close, a mere breath away. But somehow I wasn't ready to take the plunge. I cared for Harriet, but not quite enough to ask her to marry me.

We said good night, and she walked inside, disappointed, I believe. Within a short time we had split. It was all over.

So near, so very near; so close, so very close. I look back on that evening of my twenty-first birthday and feel a shudder at what might have been.

Harriet was a pleasant person—it's not as if the Lord spared me from a terrible fate. But if I had asked her to marry me and she had—as I think she was ready to do—said yes, my life would have been altogether different from what it has been. And that is to say, from what the Lord had in mind for me.

We would have married and settled down in Adelaide. I would have pursued a career in chemistry and, like my father, served the church as an active member and possibly a lay preacher. There's nothing wrong at all in such a life. Indeed, faithful lay members are the backbone of the church.

But here is the question: Would that life have been the Lord's Plan B, rather than His original purpose? Would I, by my own actions, have limited His design for my life?

My blood runs cold at the thought. Maybe it wasn't such a close call—only God knows—but I think it was. And when I think of the one whom the Lord had prepared for me as a life's companion—the one who has been, and is, best friend, counselor, helper and lover; whose breadth of mind and spiritual depth have challenged my thinking and nurtured my soul—what a tragedy if I had cut myself off from the possibility of being joined to her!

I bow in heartfelt gratitude to the One who brought me through those turbulent, decisive teen years; the One who touched me and changed me; the One who quietly revealed His plan, step by step; the One who saved me from myself.

———◆———

I am working in the lab. But the Lord is also working me over.

It's a Friday afternoon, and I am standing at a sink, cleaning up. The light shines through the window above the sink, and the Voice says, *What are you doing here?* No one else hears it. It is the Voice that we hear only within, in our soul.

I know at once what the Voice means: *It is time for you to leave this and do what I want you to do. You are to give up chemistry and go off to study to be a minister.*

For months the Lord had been implanting a divine restlessness within me. For months I had fought the Lord. How could I give up what I had spent years of study to achieve? How could I leave aging parents and family and strike out on a totally new course?

But that afternoon I gave in. "Yes, Lord, I'll do what You want me to do," I promised Him. I would enroll the next year at Avondale College and study for the ministry. Avondale is about 900 miles away from my hometown of Adelaide, but it would be the longest journey I'd ever make. Avondale meant turning away and starting over. Avondale was on the road less traveled.

The chief chemist's office was close to my lab bench. We could see him and he us through the glass by the office door. One day when he was out I slipped in and placed a letter of resignation on his bench. I observed him return to the office, pick up the letter, and begin to read it. He seemed to stare at it for a long time. Then he strode to the door.

"Come in here," he called out to me.

He was agitated. He thought I was defecting to a rival company and would take formulae with me.

"What do you want—a raise in your pay?" he demanded.

Quickly I explained that I wasn't crossing over to the opposition but was leaving chemistry to study to be a minister. It was a response he hadn't anticipated. He hardly seemed to know what to make of it.

On my last day with the firm I was told that the general manager wanted to see me. I had never met him, didn't even know what he looked like. I made my way to his office, which seemed huge.

"Well, Bill, your leaving us has created quite a stir," he said. "We thought you had a good future with us. Frankly, a lot of people think you're making a big mistake. Some even say you're crazy to do this.

"But I think I understand what's going on inside your head. I am a Presbyterian and serve as a lay preacher, so I can appreciate the way you feel."

This was an encounter I hadn't expected. This big man in the big office understood!

"Go away and study theology for a while," he continued. "But listen. After you've spent a year at that school in the bush, maybe you'll be ready to come back to us."

He put out his hand. "And you'll be welcome."

I thanked him and walked out. As I crossed the long expanse of rug from desk to door I could feel his eyes drilling into my back. And I guessed what he was thinking: *You'll be back. One year among those Adventists will be enough to make you want to return to us.*

After a year I came back to Adelaide—on summer holidays. I never went back to the lab. I was on a road that would take me far, far from all that it stood for. Farther than I could have dreamed.

CHAPTER 4

Greetings From
Southern Asia

We are all of us dreamers of dreams,
On visions our childhood is fed;
And the heart of a child is unhaunted, it seems,
By the ghosts of dreams that are dead.
—William Herbert Carruth

Reluctant I was to weigh anchors and leave Adelaide for
Avondale, but once there I threw myself in the life of the college.
In retrospect the three years at the school in the Australian bush
glow with an aura—deeply satisfying study, friends and fellowship,
and above all spiritual growth.

In those days Avondale College was a small institution with only
300 students or less. Its facilities were rudimentary, the library mod-
est, and the faculty short on advanced education. Only a couple of
them had earned doctoral degrees, but what they lacked in academic
preparation they more than compensated for by an intellectual rigor
that encouraged students to think for themselves rather than regur-
gitate the thoughts of others.

The beneficent shadow of Ellen White hung over the campus. This
pioneer of the Seventh-day Adventist Church had played a major role
in the selection of the site. When "experts" warned that the land was
useless for agriculture, she firmly counseled that this was the place the
Lord wanted the fledgling Australian church to plant its tertiary institution. The odds against the founding of a college at Avondale seemed
huge—lack of finances being the chief concern—but under the driving
force of her words and example the work went forward.

Ellen White built a home nearby, which still stands, and she took a keen interest in the new institution. According to her model, it would be a school that combined all aspects that flow together in the educated person: physical, mental, social, and spiritual. The dignity of labor would be upheld, and agriculture would be valued.

I came to Avondale some 60 years after its founding years, but the White ideals were largely intact. The college had a farm, orchards, and a dairy herd that regularly took top awards in the local agricultural shows. All students, regardless of financial assets, were required to work as part of the learning experience. With my background in chemistry I found employment in the lab of the Sanitarium Health Food Company, the large, church-owned manufacturer of breakfast foods and other products, located on the sprawling campus.

The college functioned primarily to prepare workers for the church. Theology (ministerial preparation) ranked first, followed by secondary education, elementary education, business and secretarial studies. Quite a few students attended for just a year to enjoy the fellowship and spiritual life—and to find a spouse. Students without designated majors were jokingly said to be taking the matrimonial course.

Avondale was both a physical and spiritual oasis. Access was chiefly by train to the town of Morisset and then by taxi to the college. The highway from Sydney was narrow, winding, and dangerous, and few students arrived by it. Cars were not encouraged on the campus, so you took the old train with its rocking cars and squealing rails winding its way up through the hills. Along the way the bush became more scraggly and the towns and dwellings poorer. No more cheering prospect greeted you when you got down at Morisset, a sleepy, graying town in the bush that owed its existence to an insane asylum. But at last you pulled off the highway and in through the college gate, and voilà!— what a transformation! An oasis indeed in the bush: a large, green, rolling campus, a farm, trees, and quiet beauty.

The heart of campus life was spiritual devotion, and Friday nights were the high point of the week. Students led the services, which featured a long period of singing followed by a short sermon. Meetings customarily concluded with opportunity for students to share their "testimony"—God's hand in their lives. At the conclusion of the service we spilled out onto college lawns and grouped together for earnest prayer bands. Far from the city lights the stars beamed down in dazzling clarity that made one want to reach out and grasp them. And God seemed no less close.

Across the wall of the chapel where we gathered for daily worship and instruction, the college motto was emblazoned like a banner: *For a greater vision of the world's needs.* Ellen White had predicted that from Avondale men and women would go out in the name of Jesus to serve the peoples of the South Pacific islands—and beyond. She foresaw Avondale's alumni journeying far afield, even to India.

Perhaps sparked by Ellen White's words, we students had a jocular way of addressing each other. "Greetings from Southern Asia," we'd often say.

On the rear wall of the chapel hung a plaque in memory of Norman Wiles. I felt a special attachment to him. Like me, he came from Adelaide, but unlike me, he had suffered greatly for his faith. When he decided to join the Seventh-day Adventist Church, his father, a prominent railroad official, disowned him in a towering rage. Norman eventually went to Avondale and from there to the New Hebrides (the present-day Vanuatu) as a pioneer missionary to the Big Nambus people. There he fell victim to the dread blackwater fever and died. His young wife fashioned the shroud for his burial.

Norman Wiles typified the spirit of Avondale in those days. People like him were our heroes. We would go anywhere, even to the ends of the earth, in the service of the Master.

The college was coed, but relations between the sexes were rigidly monitored. At mealtimes the young gentlemen entered the dining room through one door and the ladies through another. Monitors assigned us to tables of four, two guys and two girls. Attempts to manipulate the system so that you ended up with a special friend were frowned upon. Twice a week we could have that privilege at "ticket teas."

The most famous place on campus was The Lawn. Although large areas of mown grass beautified the college, the small square bounded by the girls' dorm, music building, and administration building held a particular attraction. Here, on benches set around the perimeter, couples were permitted to meet for private conversation. All other places were off limits. And even here, public as it was, the eagle eye of the college president looked out from an open window in the ad building.

Once a fellow student who worked on the grounds cut a beautiful rose for me to give to my lady love. I met her on the sidewalk by The Lawn. Just as I was handing here the rose, Mr. Clapham, the history teacher, happened upon us. "There's a place for that sort of thing, you know!" he snapped at me. Yes, there was an official place—and we were about three feet away from it!

As rigid and even stupid as many of the rules were—why set up a coed school and then work so mightily to keep the sexes apart?—we didn't chafe overly much. And love found a way, as it always does. Glances were exchanged, notes and messages passed by couriers; "chance" encounters, and a hundred other means that the faculty could not police, enabled relationships to bud and bloom.

It was at Avondale that I met the love of my life, and I shall always be grateful to the school in the bush for that gift. Because of credits from my degree at Adelaide University, I was able to complete the Batchelor of Arts in theology course in three years instead of the customary four. Among the new friends I made during my first year were an Ethiopian named Tshome Wagaw and Barry Taylor, a secondary education major.

Barry and I liked each other so well that we decided we'd room together the following school year. I visited him in his room several times and couldn't help noticing the large picture of a blond, bright-eyed young woman on the dressing table. She was Barry's sister,

Noelene, and she was beautiful. I was attracted to her, and I assumed that Barry displayed the photo because he felt close to his sister. Only later did I learn that the picture belonged, not to Barry, but to his roommate, Bert Gibbs!

Tshome Wagaw and I planned to sell books together in my home town of Adelaide during the summer. The school year ran February to November, to match the summer months down under. Tshome also knew the Taylor family well, and during that first year at Avondale as we became friends, he'd say to me, "Wait till you meet Barry's sister, Noelene!" I had already seen her picture, and I was waiting. And that opportunity would arrive soon, for the Taylor family lived in Melbourne, the end of the first leg of the train trip from Sydney to Adelaide. It was overnight to Melbourne, then overnight to Adelaide. Barry had duties that kept him back at the college, but he arranged for his parents to meet our train when it arrived in Melbourne, take us home to rest during the day, then put us on the evening train to Adelaide.

All that day as we rested up I was waiting for 5:00, when Noelene would come home from the school she worked at as a teacher's assistant. The hours passed slowly; then suddenly it was 5:00, and there she was. She was as lovely as her picture and then some. And also feisty. She formed her own opinions and freely expressed them. The only daughter in her family, she had learned to hold her own against three brothers in the highly chauvinistic Australian culture of that time. (In group conversations males tended to pick up from the previous male's remarks, ignoring the intervening opinion voiced by a female.)

That evening as we sat around the Taylor family table for supper, Noelene and I began the cautious exploration that leads to a relationship. After supper, when Pastor Taylor drove Tshome and me to the train station, Noelene and I sat together and talked in a more intimate setting on the back seat of the car. And as the Adelaide train pulled out, our eyes locked in a long, silent communion that said we felt mutually attracted. It was the sort of first meeting that we each felt held the seeds of bright promise. The next year would reveal whether the seeds would spring to life, for Noelene was enrolling at Avondale College in the two-year elementary education course.

Noelene arrived. We began to date. Maybe sensing that the stakes were high, we both were on our guard. The thrust and parry, the probing, the giving and receiving, the slow learning to yield self-ishness and self-centeredness and let the other be first—we had much to learn and much to unlearn. I wrote her silly poems, made her laugh; she made me think and see myself in a new light. More and more we felt we were meant for each other.

It wasn't a smooth flowering of love. We started out strongly, but after several months of steady dating we hit a plateau. Maybe we'd begun to take each other for granted. Maybe we each were re-sisting the yielding and giving that the relationship demanded if it were to continue to grow. At one point we briefly discussed break-ing up. But we prayed hard and decided to keep on dating. We felt a divine hand in what was happening.

We worked our way to a new level of knowing and appreciat-ing. At the end of the college year I took her out to the traditional performance of Handel's *Messiah*. In the midst of the music I asked her to marry me. She didn't think I was serious—I wrote a lot of fluff in the poems I sent her—and lightheartedly gave back a yes. So it was no on-your-knees, rehearsed proposal, but more a pleasant exchange during a delightful evening.

That second summer I went back to Adelaide and again sold Adventist books, but it was a struggle. The books I had to sell were old stock, plus my selling partner was a friend whose body reacted negatively to the work. He'd wake up Monday mornings with eyes red and nose running and would either stay home or quit early. Strangely, all the symptoms disappeared come Friday afternoon.

I took a week off during the summer and went to Melbourne, for Noelene's parents wanted to check out this fellow from

Adelaide. They regarded Noelene as headstrong and too ready to follow her judgment instead of theirs. Although she was now 20, they planned to have a major part in her choice of a life partner, and an aunt already had someone in mind. So I found myself treated cordially rather than welcomed. Throughout my week in the Taylor home I felt the scrutiny of the entire family.

But Noelene and I wrote often and much. We could hardly wait for the new college year to start, so that we would be together again. It would be our final year, but we had no thought that it would climax in marriage. Noelene's parents had made it clear that I should "prove" myself in the work of the church before we married; that only after a year in ministry, and preferably two years, should we even consider the possibility.

That year I made a huge mistake. Before school closed the previous year I was appointed assistant to the men's dean, which meant I would have at least half-time work on top of a heavy class load. In actuality, the responsibilities in the dorm became more demanding. The dean's health broke, and he was barely able to function. He would work for a week, then turn all his duties over to me for the following week. That became the pattern for the entire year. I found myself totally pressed from all sides as I attempted to handle the dorm and complete my graduation requirements. And, beset by cares and work, I did not foster the relationship with Noelene as I should have.

From my early years I have had the ability to focus sharply. I can see the big picture, and what needs to be done to get from here to there. This ability, which has enabled me to accomplish much in academic pursuits and in work and writing, is a two-edged sword. Its pluses come with a heavy price tag: the concentration of effort in which the mind functions like a laser leaves me emotionally drained. All too easily those I care most deeply for have had to put up with a Bill Johnsson who is but a shadow of his real self.

Only after many years did I begin to figure out the peculiar strength/weakness of my makeup. It's something I have to be aware of whenever I put out extra mental effort, such as a book manuscript like this one calls for. But way back then when Noelene and I were on the track to the altar, we both were ignorant of it. Fortunately, the Lord got us through the experience.

I came back to Avondale early in order to prepare for the new school year. Noelene returned after me—and got a shock. She arrived full of expectations, but found me detached, my head full of work. She was puzzled and disappointed. When matters didn't improve, she let me know how she felt. A wake-up call indeed! With a start, I saw how stupid I had been to let work and studies relegate her to a back seat in my life. I made adjustments; I put my priorities in order.

So our love continued to grow. Little did we know that before the year was out it would face the acid test.

At that time Avondale College had an affiliation with Pacific Union College in Angwin, California. Since Australian education operated under the British system, only universities were authorized to award degrees. So my B.A. degree in theology, like all other degrees of the college, carried the seal of the American institution.

Under the affiliation agreement, Pacific Union College assigned one of its faculty members to Avondale. During Noelene's and my time there, that person was Ivan Higgins, a big, red-faced man who had been a missionary in Southern Asia and served as president of Spicer College. At Avondale Higgins served as academic dean and registrar.

During my senior year, Higgins called Noelene and me to his office. The students who noticed it figured we were in trouble, and we had no idea of what he wanted of us. What followed left us surprised, perplexed, and troubled.

Higgins was a great storyteller, and he launched into a tale about India. He described a boarding school built at nearly 7,000 feet elevation, high on the first ridge of the Himalayas. Behind the school on slopes that reached ever higher, the eternal snows of Nepal gleamed in the stark-blue sky. Stretching out below the school, the land fell away to the plains. On a clear day, after the monsoon had scrubbed the air of dust and haze, you could see forever—100 miles or more.

As Higgins, seemingly wrapped in memories, rambled on, Noelene and I wondered why he was telling us all this. This school for missionaries' kids—where the trees were covered in ferns during the monsoon, where you could see the clouds form beneath you, where the rhododendrons bloomed wild on the hillside—seemed a fascinating place, but so what?

Higgins paused. Then, looking us in the eye, he said, "They need a boy's preceptor [dormitory dean] and a music teacher at the school. A call will be coming for you both."

We were stunned, hardly daring to believe what we heard. At one level his words made sense. I was assistant to the men's dean, and along with Noelene's studies in elementary education she was preparing for the Sydney Conservatorium's examinations in piano. We felt the need. But what about the rest? An official church call? *To India?*

How would Noelene's parents react to that possibility? And what about my parents? My father was in his 70s, my mother four years younger—it would be a wrench for them.

We had not made application for mission service. We had never thought of the possibility, let alone discussed it together. The prospect that suddenly opened before us was at once exciting and daunting. Against all expectations we could marry after graduation instead of having to wait for one or two years, but the obstacles and challenges that lay ahead loomed very large.

Higgins, of course, had been in touch with leaders of the church in Southern Asia. They had written to him about the staff needs at Vincent Hill School and he had recommended Noelene and me. We weren't married, not even engaged to be married, but it was as obvious to Higgins as to others on the campus that we were in love and planned to marry.

Although the meeting with Higgins took us totally by surprise, it did not take Noelene and me long to decide that yes, we should accept the call to India. For me the decision seemed relatively straightforward: in leaving chemistry and home, I had made a commitment to the Lord to be His servant, to go or to stay, to speak or to be silent as He directed. Noelene had not experienced a parallel break, so the way ahead was not as clear to her. Nevertheless, out of her love for me she soon decided that she would go with me to India if that is where the Lord wanted us to be.

At this point, not long after the meeting with Higgins, we decided on a course of action that, while well intended, had very negative consequences.

Noelene's father was a minister, and the children had grown up praying for the church's missionaries. Further, her parents had impressed on the children never to refuse a request for service officially voted by church administrators—a "call." A call from "the church" was a call from God and not to be treated lightly. So, we reasoned, we should wait until we actually received the letter of call before we told her parents. Faced with the call, they would surely give their blessing.

Higgins had indicated that the leaders in Southern Asia were planning to issue the call; perhaps they had already done so. It would be only a short time before we received it. We decided that we would tell no one about the meeting with Higgins—not even Noelene's brother Barry—until the call came.

Problem: the call didn't come. Days passed into weeks, and weeks into months. Still no call. What had happened?

Higgins was puzzled. "Have you heard from Southern Asia?" he would ask us.

"I don't understand why you haven't received the call," he told us at last. "The Southern Asia Division voted to call you both to India some time ago. You should hear from the brethren any day."

But we didn't—not a word. As the months dragged on, Noelene and I became increasingly perplexed. The call Higgins was so sure of meant far more than leaving our homeland for a far-off field. It meant plans for a wedding. But before the wedding we faced discussions with Noelene's parents that we sensed might prove to be difficult.

And we continued to wait.

In fact, the official call had come. Following church protocol, leaders in Southern Asia had sent the letter of call to church headquarters in Australia for it to be forwarded to us. And there it sat for several months. The leaders in Australia may have been miffed that two of their future workers were being called to go to India when they hadn't even applied for mission service, or they may simply have figured that it wasn't a good idea for us to receive the call in the middle of the school year. For whatever reason, they decided to send on the call only when the others who would be graduating received their calls—which would be late October.

But Noelene and I were sitting on a time bomb. Every day that passed increased the odds that the whole matter would come out. We should have told our parents what was in the wind, but we kept hoping and expecting to receive the call any day, and then the news would be more palatable.

Inevitably, word leaked out. The Avondale campus began to buzz with a rumor that two of the upcoming graduates were being called to India. Noelene's brother Barry heard the buzz and, noticing the secretiveness of Noelene's and my conversations, put two and two together. He went to Higgins and confirmed his suspicions.

And the fat was in the fire.

"Will you tell Mum and Dad, or shall I?" he asked Noelene. We said we'd give them the news.

And so I wrote a letter to them that I thought would make the case and explain the reasons we had not kept them informed of developments. I was naive. They were furious—with Noelene, with Higgins for suggesting our names to the Southern Asia Division, and most of all with me. I had wormed my way into Noelene's affections and wanted to snatch her away from them and take her to a distant and dangerous land. I had ignored protocol and asked her to marry me without first gaining their consent.

I tried to apologize, but they refused to accept it. Nor could Noelene get through to them, for they saw her as complicit in my actions. This was the latest and worst case of her disregard for their counsel over the years.

Eventually I decided that enough was enough. Granted that we hadn't handled the matter as well as we might have, but our motives had been honorable. After all, we weren't teenagers. I was 25, and Noelene was just shy of her twenty-first birthday. And there was a deeper, overriding factor that strengthened my will: three years before, I had made the break with home and family to go wherever the Lord directed. And in my soul His direction now pointed to India.

Noelene went through a more difficult process before she arrived at peace of mind. She agonized with the Lord, trying to sort out her motives and emotions. The call and her marriage to me were bound up in one package. Knowing that I felt convinced that we should accept the call, she wrestled with knowing if it was God's will for her to marry me and accompany me to India against the strong counsels of her family.

Looking back on those difficult days, the what ifs are intriguing. If she had decided she would obey her parents' wishes and not go to India, would our relationship have weathered the storm? How could I, who had felt such a strong sense of the Lord's guidance in my life and felt it again at this time, have handled a refusal of what I was convinced was a divine commission?

Noelene wrestled with the Lord and came to the place of peace. In spite of the strenuous objections of those dear to her—well-meaning, good people who nevertheless viewed her contemplated actions as disobedience to parents, and told her so—she would marry me and go with me to India. It was a decision that brought her into a close relationship with the Lord and one that has led her increasingly over the years to believe in, practice, and promote the power of personal prayer.

And it was a decision that cemented her love to me. In India it would be just her and me. There would be no mother to turn to, no home to come back to. We would have only each other and the Lord. Our love would have to see us through whatever life threw at us in that far-off land.

We encountered mixed reactions to our decision. On campus our fellow students generally welcomed it and were happy for us. Like us, they were dreamers, captured by a greater vision of the world's needs. But older folks tended to see matters differently. The pastor of my home church in Adelaide shook his head in concern. "You'll be forgotten over there in the mission field," he warned. "When you come back to Australia, there'll be no place for you in the work." Others related experiences of missionaries in India who had broken down in health and could not function successfully when they had completed their term of service.

We listened respectfully but were little moved by the naysayers. The Lord gave us a robust optimism that made us confident that we could meet whatever circumstances came our way, either in India or after India. What to some seemed unwise, even folly or impossible, to us seemed something to be embraced. The Lord would be with us; we would be in His hands. That was all that mattered.

And then we received the call. Not in late October, as the church leaders planned, but at the beginning of September. It came to us because of a typing error.

I received a letter with the Australasian Division return address and, heart racing, tore it open. Inside was a letter to the college president, Gordon McDowell, instructing him to give the enclosed letter of call to Noelene and me when the other students received their appointments in October. But the office secretary—bless her!—typed my name instead of McDowell's on the envelope!

I went to McDowell's office. "We have received the call we have been expecting," I told him.

He looked startled. "Oh, you did, did you?"

It was the first day of spring down under. The same day Noelene and I announced our engagement. A few days later we obtained special dispensation to go to Sydney. I bought her the gold watch she picked out and put it on her wrist. We wandered through the city streets and out to the beautiful park alongside the span of the Harbour Bridge, where we sat on the green slope as boats and ferries plied below us. It was a magical day that wiped clean all the uncertainties and pain of the previous months.

The next three months were a blur. So much to do: studies to complete, preparations for setting up home in India, and the wedding. Church officials in India wanted us to get there as soon as possible, and put us on the payroll starting December 1.

We graduated from Avondale in mid-November.

We wed December 21.

We sailed for India on January 10.

I went home to Adelaide after graduation. We would be married in the Nunawading church in the city of Melbourne, so I arranged to get the necessary inoculations for India while at home. Typhoid, cholera, smallpox—it would be our first experience of what would become a recurring feature of life in India.

When I went to the family doctor's office for the smallpox vaccination, I learned that our regular doctor was away on leave. An intern was filling in. He hadn't given vaccinations, and seemed tentative. Some days later, when I went back to have him sign the yellow medical card, he announced that the vaccination hadn't "taken."

"Let's try this again," he said. Jab, jab, jab on my left arm.

"Let's be quite sure it 'takes' this time." Jab, jab, jab.

It took, and he signed the card.

The wedding was to be on a Monday evening. I took the train to Melbourne a few days earlier and allowed myself the luxury of a "sleeper" compartment so as to arrive fresh for meeting Noelene's friends and family. But I couldn't sleep. I tossed all night. I remember the car attendant coming by in the night and asking if I needed anything.

I arrived in Melbourne feeling lousy. As Noelene and I walked the streets making last-minute purchases, I felt worse and worse.

I stayed at the home of my sister Gwen, a trained nurse. That Friday night she looked at me closely and sent me to bed. After a bit she came in with a thermometer.

"I thought so," she said as she read my temperature. It was more than 104 degrees.

She looked at my left arm—angry red and swollen around the smallpox vaccination. That arm would continue to swell for several weeks. On the boat to India I could barely get a shirt sleeve over it.

Sabbath was to have been Noelene's "show-me-off" day at her church. Instead I spent it sweating and tossing in bed.

By Sunday evening the fever broke, and we were able to proceed with the wedding rehearsal as planned. But Noelene's parents still were not reconciled to our getting married. The evening of the rehearsal her father, who was to officiate at the service, took Noelene aside. "Are you sure you want to go ahead with this wedding?" he wanted to know.

It was the only cloud on an otherwise wonderful day. The bride looked stunning, and the dear people who filled the church showered us with love and goodwill. The bridegroom looked a bit gaunt, with dark shadows not quite faded under his eyes, but he survived the big day. (My mother had fattened me up for the wedding, but the smallpox reaction brought my weight down to 139 pounds.)

Our ship sailed from Melbourne, with stops in Adelaide and Fremantle, the port near Perth in Western Australia. As we prepared to board from the final stop in our native land, I plucked some eucalyptus leaves and put them in the pocket of the navy blue blazer I was wearing. They stayed there for several years, turning gray but still bearing the distinctive smell of Oz.

It would be more than five years before we would see Australia and any of our loved ones again. When we came home on furlough, we had a 4-year-old son and a daughter two years younger. That was the first time our parents saw their grandchildren. Our going to India meant a big sacrifice for them.

On that first furlough Noelene's dad still expressed reservations about our accepting the call to Southern Asia. "Only eternity will tell if it was really the Lord's will," he said.

Slowly, however, as the years passed he and I grew closer. He read widely; we had much to share with each other. We became good friends as his pride in us and our service increased.

CHAPTER 5

Under the Indian Sun

Oh, East is East, and West is West,
And never the twain shall meet,
Till Earth and Sky stand presently
At God's great Judgment Seat.
—Rudyard Kipling

No one is neutral about India: you either love the country, or you hate it. If you love it, you will want to return. If you hate it, nothing will drag you back.

We stayed 15½ years. We loved India. Soon after we arrived another missionary couple who had just arrived quit after only five days. The wife found it all too much. She didn't stop crying the whole time she was in India.

Everything about India is different—the vast numbers of people, the heat, the smells, the beggars. You're overwhelmed with culture shock. You have landed in a sea of surging taxis, bicycles, bullock carts, pedestrians—and holy cows wandering aimlessly, kings of the road. A babble of sounds—strange languages mixed with something that sounds like English—assaults your ears. You see shop signs in familiar letters but also in scripts that dangle from horizontal lines or wiggle and curl. Street hawkers thrust baubles in your face. Lepers, stumps of hands and feet covered in filthy rags, hold out cans imploringly. Flies cover the fruit and pastries on roadside stands.

India is shocking.

And yet—India is beautiful.

Color strikes your eye at every turn—saris flashing reds and gold; men in exotic headgear; trees that blaze yellow, orange, red, blue.

Nature works on a vast scale here. The highest mountains on earth, the Himalayas—literally "place of snow"—magnificent, mind-stopping. Mighty rivers—Brahmaputra, Ganges, Jumna. Deserts bake and boil under the fierce power of the sun; lush plains of the Punjab yield an abundant harvest of wheat, and Andhra rice fields produce a bounty of plenty.

India has only two seasons: the wet and the dry. Or perhaps three: the wet, the cool (a relative term), and the dry. All life here is a gift of the monsoon. It rains only once a year, but it rains for two or three months almost nonstop.

After the annual deluge, which ends in September, the land slowly dries out. The color green fades to yellow, and then disappears. As month follows month, the plains sizzle and burn. The ground cracks. The air grows hotter, day and night. Man and beast long for the gift of life to return.

It is on the way. The meteorologists track it; predict when it will reach the southern tip of India, then Bombay, then Delhi as it marches inexorably northward. The weather maps show it: a sharp line, a moving line, drawn across the country. From an airplane you see it: to the south, a dense sea of white; to the north, clear sky.

Ahead of the monsoon, the thirsty land cries out for breath. Behind it, water in the streets runs ankle-deep and streams swell into torrents. It comes with wind, thunder, and lightning—a few drops of dirty water, then a relentless drumming, drumming, drumming. You dash out into the downpour and let the gift of life course through your hair, down your face, over your whole body.

But nature works on a vast scale here. For some Indians, the monsoon brings overabundance: floods, homes swept away, lives swept away. For others the monsoon behaves in a fickle manner, arriving late or not at all. Which means the year ahead will yield little or no crop, only poverty and hungry stomachs.

Every year, the same as everybody else, we counted time by the monsoon, how many days before it would arrive, how long before it would retreat whence it came and the skies would be blue and clear over a land sparkling emerald green and coursing with rivulets. And every year in the long days of oppressive waiting, we observed the gift of the heat: the most colorful trees bloomed in the midst of summer. The hotter and drier, the more glorious the reds, yellows, and oranges. Leaves might be few, but blossoms were abundant.

India shocks. India terrifies. But India amazes with its beauty.

Most beautiful of all India's wonders are its people. Indians are a gentle people, generous and hospitable, kind to the stranger and visitor. The simple home may have few comforts, but the hosts bring out all it holds to make you feel welcome.

And Indians love humor. They enjoy jokes and pranks, tall stories. They love to dress up and perform. It's no surprise that their movie industry, centered in Bombay's Bollywood, is the world's largest.

India is an ancient land. For thousands of years sages have pondered the enigma of human existence: life and death, wealth and poverty, health and sickness. Every person, whether learned or illiterate, is a philosopher here.

The religions of humanity spring from two fountainheads. One fountainhead is the Abrahamic, from whence issued Judaism and Christianity and then, 600 years after Jesus, Islam.

The other fountainhead is the Indian, where Hinduism, greatly influenced by nature's mighty display, arose. With its plethora of deities and manifold philosophies, Hinduism gave its answer to the big questions: in unyielding justice (karma) and reincarnation, with the caste system as the social component. Then, in due course, two reform movements arose within Hinduism, one destined to become a world religion in its own right, the other a small religion confined to India itself—Buddhism and Jainism.

But India's role as a mother of religions was not yet exhausted.

When, in the seventh century A.D., Arab invaders carrying the new religion of Islam swept into Persia, the remnants of the Zoroastrian faith sought refuge in India. They continue there to this day, the Parsees, comparatively few in numbers but disproportionately influential as leaders in commerce, the military, and the arts.

And still one more religion: 800 years ago another revolt against the domination of the priestly caste, the Brahmans, took place. Out of it arose Sikhism, a blend of Hinduism and Islam. (The Sikhs are recognized by the turban that covers hair and beard—strictly observant males never cut their hair.)

We arrived in India fresh out of school, just married. No preparation for service in a foreign country, no courses, no reading— zilch, zero.

We arrived with stars in our eyes. Forget that India, purportedly first evangelized by the apostle Thomas, had resisted all efforts by Christian emissaries. Forget that Adventist workers had toiled since the 1890s to raise up a church of less than 20,000 members. We would go forth in Jesus' name to conquer, to succeed where others had failed.

We had much to learn.

Our ship docked in Bombay, now called Mumbai, in the wee hours of the morning. We awakened to the sound of metal clanging as cargo was unloaded and a foul odor assailing our senses. Is this the smell of India we'd heard about? we wondered. But soon we learned that the vile stench came from sheep's hides that had been shipped with us from Australia.

As we prepared to disembark, someone thrust customs papers in our hands. Before we had a chance to fill them out, a White man came hurrying to meet us.

"Don't write anything!" he urged us, taking the papers from us.

He introduced himself as Alf Johnson, assistant treasurer of the Southern Asia Division. He had come to help us clear customs—a process that opened up a new disturbing world to us.

Johnson explained that the customs officials had the power to impose exorbitant duties. They could keep your goods bottled up for as long as they chose. They worked on the premise that all passengers intentionally understated the value of their possessions. It was a shady game, and innocents like us could land in big trouble if we tried to handle the clearance of our goods by ourselves.

Before we left Australia we had received an outfitting allowance and had spent it on a few basic items—a bed, a small refrigerator, two comfortable chairs, a small washing machine and a cooking range. We ordered from a catalogue, and the goods were sent directly to the ship. Now, on the dock, we saw an assortment of boxes with our name on them. A bed spring lay naked, without wrapping, a label designating it as belonging to us.

We tried to figure out what each box contained.

"What's in that?" asked the customs officer.

"That must be our refrigerator."

"And what about that?"

"Don't know—maybe *that's* the refrigerator."

We let Alf Johnson take charge, and eventually, after what seemed a lot of talking, he arrived at an amount with the official, paid the bill, and we were out of there.

Our goods, which looked puny and forlorn on the docks, would be trucked to the far north of India. They would eventually arrive at our home on the backs of coolies who hauled them over the mountain.

And then we'd be in for a surprise. Only a few items from our list would make it to our door. We would learn that a large part of that puny shipment that bore our name wasn't ours at all—it belonged to other missionaries who had sent in orders to Australia for foodstuffs and so on. No wonder we had a difficult time figuring out the contents of the boxes on the dock. The items missing from our list hadn't made it to the ship on time. Only five or six months later did they arrive by a different vessel.

The shady world of customs clearance introduced us to a society that in certain respects operated in very different ways from the one we had left. In short, it functioned by "money under the table." From that first day in India I felt uncomfortable with it, and although Noelene and I made huge adjustments to life in the new land until we felt happy and at home, we never outgrew our unease with this aspect of life.

But the issue one faced was this. How can one function—do what needs to be done—without in some measure accommodating to the prevailing modus operandi? I remember well the time that, at short notice, I was asked to speak for the commencement services of the nurses' training school at Nuzvid Memorial Hospital in south India. We were teaching at Spicer College, and the trip would entail a long journey by train. I went to the railway station and asked the clerk to sell me a ticket. He thumbed through a large, dog-eared ledger, going back and forth.

"Sorry, sahib; no place available."

The assistant business manager of the college, maybe anticipating the scene, had accompanied me to the station. "Please take another look," he said to the clerk as, almost unnoticed, he slid a five-rupee note under the ledger.

The clerk thumbed back and forth, back and forth.

"Sahib, one seat! I have found a seat for you!"

I had my ride. But I felt somehow sullied.

It's easy for those of us from the West to look down on other cultures because they operate from norms different from ours. Before we go down that road, however, I suggest we stand back and turn the spotlight on our own society. Doesn't it also operate on two levels—the official level and an under-the-table level? Aren't tips, "service" fees and "right connections" really a more sophisticated version of what I encountered at the train station? And haven't you noticed: politicians never seem to leave office poorer than they arrived! Somehow, out of those not-so-hefty salaries, they manage to do very well for themselves.

———◆———

When we arrived in India in 1960, the Southern Asia Division consisted of India, Pakistan (both East and West—East would split off later to form Bangladesh), Ceylon (now Sri Lanka), and Burma (now Myanmar). There were a lot of missionaries—more than 100—and they ran the show. All administrative positions, at all levels, were in the hands of foreigners.

It was a byword that new missionaries never ended up at the post they were called to. Before they arrived, a new need would arise, and they would be shunted elsewhere.

We were the exception. We were called to Vincent Hill School, and to Vincent Hill we went. I worked as Bible teacher and dean in the boys' hostel. Noelene served as matron for the younger boys and piano teacher.

Vincent Hill had opened in the early 1900s as a church-owned boarding school for the children of missionaries and Anglo-Indians, a community that had given substantially toward the founding of the school. Situated on the first ridge of the Himalayas at 6,500 feet, the school was above the malaria line. It was at the end of the town of Mussoorie, a long, sprawling, up-and-down settlement that featured several high-class schools and attracted many tourists during the hot summer months.

It was a grand, wild location. To the north the mighty mountains marched row on row ever higher to the eternal snows of Tibet. Valleys dropped steeply away thousands of feet. To the south the plains of India stretched on and on to the horizon, farther than the eye could see.

Access to Vincent Hill School was by train, bus, and foot—train from Delhi to Dehra Dun, at the foot of the mountains; bus on the long, winding switchback road to Mussoorie; then by foot up the road to the top of Vincent Hill and down to the school several hundred feet below. The school owned no motorized vehicles. There was no accessible road to the school.

The school had been cut from the rock. Everything was up or down. In the center was a large flat area holding the administration building, girls' dorm, cafeteria, and a play area. Up and down from the center were small cuts for staff housing. At the very bottom, on another large cut, was the boys' dormitory. Our apartment was in one corner of it.

When Noelene and I came to Vincent Hill, the school had just 100 students, all boarding. They came from missionary families scattered across India, Pakistan, Ceylon, and Burma; also from African and eastern and southwestern Asia, plus a few from America. The school had a reputation for academic excellence. One year the average IQ tested at 117.

We had the great good fortune to commence our work for the church under a prince. Principal of the school Myrl O. Manley was a person of unswerving integrity. Tall and straight, he looked at you with a direct gaze that told you he meant what he said. He was always on duty, day and night; he rarely left the hillside to attend committees. He ran a taut, tight ship that earned the respect of everyone, teachers and students, and that made Vincent Hill one of the denomination's outstanding institutions.

Pastor Manley had a serious demeanor, but he loved the students intensely, always seeking their best good. I saw that demonstrated vividly when Richard Hammill, then of the General Conference Education Department, came on an inspection. At the end of the visit Hammill met with Manley and the staff in the principal's office. What we didn't know was that someone had hung a pair of red panties on the outside knob of the closed door. Manley happened to leave the room for something. He saw the panties and without breaking stride shoved them in his jacket pocket. No one—not Hammill or any of us—knew what had happened.

After Hammill left the campus, Manley soon found out who had hung the panties on the door and the girl who had supplied them to him. Then Manley told just two other people—the girls' dean, Clara Hawes, and me. "If I take this to the whole staff," he said, "some of them will demand that they [the offenders] be sent home." So the three of us decided on an appropriate discipline, which was administered quietly.

Our lives were full at Vincent Hill. They totally revolved around the students: morning and evening worships, teaching classes, supervising the work detail, playing with them, hiking. We went into the town only on boys' day, once a week. A full year and a half passed before someone filled in for us to give us a weekend away from the campus.

I was happy—deliriously happy. "Why is Mr. Johnsson always smiling?" a student asked Noelene. Noelene, 21, was only a few years senior to the oldest girls and looked younger than some of them. Once visiting parents complained to Pastor Manley that he was allowing boys and girls to walk hand in hand up the road. He explained that the couple they had seen weren't students!

For many months people called us the "honeymoon couple." That ceased when it became obvious that Noelene was pregnant.

Mussoorie boasted a government hospital and a small mission hospital with an American doctor. We liked what we saw in the latter, but there was a problem—our baby was due January 27, and the mission hospital closed during the winter months. We learned that in Simla—the summer capital of the nation during the raj—the Adventist Church ran a hospital, so we made arrangements to go there for the delivery of our firstborn.

As the crow flies Simla wasn't far away, but getting there from Mussoorie was something else. We walked over the hill and into Mussoorie, took a taxi to Dehra Dun and then the train to Delhi, where we overnighted. Then another train to the foot of the mountains and finally a narrow-gauge train up to Simla.

The doctors at the hospital, a husband-wife team, welcomed us warmly. But they explained that a hitch had developed. Queen Elizabeth was visiting India, and they had received an invitation to attend a garden party in New Delhi on Republic Day, January 26. They wanted to attend the function, but of course Noelene and the baby had to be given first consideration. Their plan? The baby was almost due, so they would admit Noelene into the hospital and induce labor.

They tried and tried. Noelene went through days of false labor, but no baby. The doctors decided that there'd be no baby for at least another week, discharged Noelene, and left for New Delhi.

Not long after they left, Noelene began having contractions. One evening she packed a bag and said, "I think you'd better stay with me at the hospital tonight." That night the contractions came stronger and closer. About 6:00 the next morning the two American nurses who were left in charge of the hospital moved Noelene to the delivery room. One had been a county nurse in Florida, but neither was trained as a midwife.

The unheated delivery room was deathly cold. We could see snow falling, building up. And Noelene was locked in a terrible struggle to bring new life into the world. Exhausted by the days of induced labor, she hadn't the strength to give birth.

The hours wore on, all through the morning. The snow rose higher. "Push! Push!" the nurses kept telling her. But her strength was spent. Try as she might, the baby wouldn't come.

About 1:00 p.m. the nurses, now anxious, began to discuss calling for a doctor from another hospital. Then suddenly, with an anguished cry, Noelene made one more effort, and the baby was delivered.

He was blue, and his head, so long in the birth canal, was elongated. For a brief moment he remained silent; then the nurse slapped his back, and he broke into a pathetic (to us, joyful) cry.

Many years later I referred briefly in a book to Terry's difficult birth. Out of the blue came a letter from Hailey Thomas, the Florida nurse. "Could this be the same baby boy that was born in Simla?" she asked. "I was concerned about him. For some years I made discreet inquiries to learn if he had been affected, but was told he was normal."

Normal? I would say so. Terry graduated with honors from Andrews University and earned a master's degree in international business studies from the University of South Carolina. From there he went immediately into the employ of General Motors, where currently he serves as a vice president.

But when I think of that cold delivery room in Simla long ago, my blood turns to ice. Noelene and I, young and naive, knew so little of the perils of the situation. Only gradually, after many years, did we begin to grasp the extent of the Lord's deliverance.

Myrl Manley and his gracious wife, Beth, returned to the United States after our second year at Vincent Hill School. They had been like parents to Noelene and me, and we missed them keenly. And our thinking began to change.

We loved our work at Vincent Hill, but, important as it was, we wanted to work among the people of India. Keenly conscious of a sense of calling to the ministry, I feared that I might be sidetracked from it. Besides, I had studied Hindi and wanted to put the new skill into practice. Toward the end of our third year in the mountains we wrote to leaders at church headquarters in Poona requesting a new assignment that would allow us to minister to the people of India.

The church leaders took note, and then an action that totally surprised us. We expected to be given pastoral or evangelistic work. Instead, they directed us to relocate to Spicer College for full-time teaching of Bible and religion courses.

I could hardly believe the news. I loved study, and secretly harbored the hope that one day I might be given the opportunity to teach college religion courses. But I was sure that that dream, if it ever came to pass, would certainly be many years away, and only after I had done further study. Here I was, still in my 20s and with only a B.A. degree, with the dream suddenly realized!

———————◆————

We came to Spicer College at an exciting time in its history. A new, young president, Maliakal E. Cherian, had just been elected, and he had a vision of great things for the college—to make it a premium institution, one of such excellence that it would win recognition in its own right from the educational authorities of India.

India follows the British system, which ties higher education to the universities. They alone have the authority to grant degrees. Colleges affiliate with a university and prepare students for the examinations set by the university. Those colleges that attempt to follow their own curriculum and award degrees suffer the stigma that their degrees are not recognized in the marketplace or for further study.

Cherian could have made Spicer a college of Poona University, which adjoined the college property, and thereby have its students receive recognized degrees. That, however, would mean following the university's curriculum. But Cherian wanted Spicer to preserve its own unique course of study, with Bible and religion classes an integral part.

It was a bold vision. Spicer's dynamic and the quality of its graduates would have to be of such a caliber that they could not be denied recognition.

A leader of strong mind and infectious enthusiasm, Cherian poured himself into the work. He toiled long hours; we caught his vision and willingly toiled with him. Although he was a strong nationalist, he made the expatriate faculty feel at home. Indian, American, British, Canadian, Australian—it didn't matter to him as long as you rolled up your sleeves and got the job done.

I admired Cherian. I have never worked for a more visionary boss. A couple of us younger faculty became known as the "young Turks" because we were always pushing for faster progress. He enjoyed us—

enjoyed verbal sparring, enjoyed a challenge to the status quo.

Cherian was a man of great grace—he had to have been to have put up with the realities of the church's pay scale. In those days missionaries were reimbursed on a totally separate basis from nationals, and the disparity was huge. Here I was, a junior professor with only a bachelor's degree. Cherian was the college president with a Ph.D. and two master's degrees. But my paycheck was much larger than his! The injustice must have stung, but whatever his feelings, I never heard him voice them on the campus.

Cherian toiled ceaselessly, on and off campus. He cultivated relations with Poona University and the leaders of government at the state and national level. He invited them to visit the campus, to see for themselves the quality of the education that Spicer offered. And slowly he began to see breakthroughs. Spicer graduates were admitted for master's degrees, then doctoral degrees, at Poona University, and then at other universities. Spicer had won de facto recognition of its programs.

But Cherian wanted more. He dreamed of the day that Spicer College would be granted the status of an independent, degree-conferring university. He never gave up the dream, even after he left the college to become president of the Southern Asia Division. Cherian is gone now, but his vision for Spicer still hangs in the air, awaiting fulfillment.

—•◆•—

I sat with a friend in a large meeting in the city of Indore in central India. Jawaharlal Nehru, the prime minister, was addressing thousands of people At one point Nehru, who had been speaking in Hindi, looked straight at us and switched to English, then went back to Hindi.

Our years in India profoundly changed Noelene and me: we became world persons. Slowly, gradually, I came to see an ugly side of me, one that I would have denied. I was a racist. No, not toward all people with dark skin—one of my close friends at Avondale College was an

Ethiopian—but toward the Aboriginal peoples of my native land. Like those around me, I grew up thinking of them as not fully human.

In India, with White faces a small minority, I discovered the ugly me and felt ashamed. I will be forever grateful for that discovery.

But there was more—much more—to learn.

I loved college teaching, but pretty soon realized that if it was to be my life, I needed to qualify myself academically—which meant not just a master's degree but a Ph.D.

On our first furlough we were granted study leave at Andrews University. There at the seminary I completed an M.A. in theology. We returned to Spicer, and during the next four years I studied in my spare time on a Bachelor of Divinity degree as an external student of London University. (In the U.S. the B.D. degree is designated the M.Div.) Now with M.A. and B.D. degrees under my belt, I felt ready to tackle the Ph.D. We asked the division for a leave of absence. Instead they voted to sponsor us for doctoral studies.

So we arrived in August 1970 in Nashville, Tennessee, where I had been admitted to the doctoral program in New Testament studies at Vanderbilt University. I came eager to learn—but also eager to finish in the shortest possible time. The program was rigorous: coursework, comprehensive examinations, approval of a dissertation topic, researching the topic, and—finally—oral defense of the dissertation. The program, start to finish, customarily took about eight years.

I cannot here relate the series of divine serendipities that came to me at Vanderbilt—how the foreign language requirements (German and French) were met in stride, how the authorities allowed me to sit the comprehensive exams out of turn, how I was permitted to begin work on the dissertation before all required coursework was completed, and more! Suffice it to say that what seemed impossible turned, under the Lord's hand, into reality. We left Nashville on March 1, 1973, with the oral defense passed and the dissertation topic approved and handed in—just two and a half years from our arrival.

It still doesn't seem possible. But the impossible is what this book is all about.

—————◆◆◆—————

Noelene and I returned to India determined to do things differently. We would not—could not—go back to the way we had lived before.

In the United States we had been forced to confront the evil of segregation. The members at First church in Nashville had welcomed us most graciously—but the church was all White. Black Adventists who showed up on Sabbath mornings were directed to a church at which they would "feel at home." At Vanderbilt integration had arrived only a few years earlier, and the divinity school had led the way.

In Nashville Noelene and I reflected on our life at Spicer College. The missionaries frequently came together for potluck dinners, but they were Whites-only affairs. Most Sabbath afternoons after church we'd gather in the shaded driveway of a teacher's home and lay out a big spread. We'd sit around for hours swapping stories while students and national teachers went out on missionary activities. Christmas Day was a big event. A procession of cars carrying foreigners left campus and headed out to the Poona Boat Club, where we'd spend the day in festivities. In the evening, faculty and students saw the line of cars returning to the campus.

But now there was no way we could go back to that life. We let it be known that we would not come to potlucks unless they were opened to all. And no more exclusive Christmas Days at the boat club.

Our stand didn't make us popular with some expatriates, but quite soon things changed. Others had begun to feel the same way we did. The time was ripe to leave the old ways behind.

—————◆◆◆—————

We had been back in India a little more than a year when we received a letter from Richard Hammill, president of Andrews

University. "By now you will have received the call to teach at the seminary . . ." it read. We knew nothing about it. In an eerie echo of the circumstances of our original call to India, the division—now Southern Asia—had decided to sit on the call.

The call to Andrews put us in a quandary. We loved India, we loved Spicer College, and we loved the students. But our children, both born in India, were growing up, and they needed to develop a clear sense of where they belonged.

What to do? Then something happened that settled the matter for us.

During the year before, not long after our return from America, a strike had broken out on campus. Students took over, shutting everything down. The police who were called in proved ineffective. For a week all classes were suspended. It was a time of deep tension, including some violence.

The strike was broken, but it left angry memories. One year later—to the day—posters sprang up around the campus. They called on the administration to resign and, alarmingly, for me to be made president.

Immediately I knew what we should do. I would have no part in any development that would replace a national leader with a missionary. I had strong convictions on this matter and had made no secret of them in private and in public.

The time had come. Time to move on. We had come on time; we would leave on time.

Leaving India wasn't easy. The land and its peoples had become part of us, and always will be. A delegation of students came to our home, begging us to stay just one more year until they graduated. It was hard to tell them no.

You either love India or hate it. We loved it. I have been back many times and would go again at the drop of a hat.

Noelene and I are forever grateful to India and its peoples.

CHAPTER 6

Camelot

A little learning is a dangerous thing;
drink deep, or taste not the Pierian spring.
—Alexander Pope

The years at the Seventh-day Adventist Theological Seminary on the campus of Andrews University were my Camelot. I thought I would be there forever, or until they wheeled me out.

I taught in Adventist schools for 20 years—secondary, college, seminary—and loved it all. There was never a class I was glad to see behind me. Some days, of course, left plenty to be desired, but in the next class the dynamic would spring back. Every fall, the night before classes started, I tossed in bed, wondering, eager to meet the new faces that the morning would bring.

Apart from courses in archaeology, over the years I taught pretty well all that the seminary bulletin offered in New Testament. That meant that each year I had new preparations, new material to master and to figure how to present most effectively. It's been my practice to keep Saturday nights free from work—even when facing major examinations—but I broke that rule at the seminary. In the first years, dealing with multiple preparations each semester, I often went to my little office in the seminary building after Sabbath and lovingly worked late.

When I joined the faculty, famed archaeologist Seigfried Horn was dean of the seminary. I had sat in his classes and, like the whole community, admired and revered him. When as a new faculty member, I addressed him as Dr. Horn, he cut me short. "Now, Bill, we're colleagues. You must call me Seigfried." I tried, but could not—the personal form of address stuck in my throat.

Horn, great scholar that he was, didn't care for administration, but out of loyalty to his church he accepted the dean's post when requested. At the earliest opportunity, however, he retired and resumed the life of study. He was succeeded by Tom Blincoe, who had worked with Horn as assistant dean handling student affairs.

Tom Blincoe and I became more than colleagues; we were friends. His son, Tommy, and our son, Terry, were in the same year in academy, and the families became thrown together. Tom Blincoe was a person of love and piety—if ever someone qualified to be called "good," it was he. I appreciated him dearly and grew to love him. After a while, realizing that he needed help with his office load, he requested the Andrews board to appoint an associate dean to handle the academic side while he continued to guide student affairs. The lot fell to me, so for my last two years at the seminary Tom and I worked together even more closely.

Tom Blincoe—what a prince! What a privilege to have known him as a friend, colleague, and confidant.

On the home front, we were all together as a family—it would be the last years, although we didn't realize it. Terry was in academy and Julie in middle school. Noelene studied at Andrews and completed a master's degree in teaching, then found employment in the local school system. We lived just a mile from the campus, and I often walked to and from classes.

I loved it. I thought we would be there forever. Camelot.

Not quite—I never did make peace with the Michigan winters. I am a summer person. I love blue skies and heat. Andrews University, so close to Lake Michigan, gets lots of gray skies—and snow dumped by the winds that cross the lake and fill with moisture. One January I shoveled snow every single day of the month—and we had a long driveway. The snow piled up on either side and on the streets, until driving was like navigating between high white walls. But if you can't beat 'em, join 'em. By the fifth winter I began to take up cross-country skiing, and even went into a store to buy my own skis. They didn't have what I was looking for, so I walked out. And that was the end of my cross-country skiing.

———◦◆◦———

The Seminary bulletin listed two courses on the book of Hebrews, one on exegesis, the other on the theology of the book. Before I joined the faculty, neither course had been offered for a couple years. I immediately took over both. Many students were interested in the subject matter and signed up for them.

This biblical book has played a major role in my life and work. I have spent more time reflecting on it and seeking to unlock its reasoning than on any other portion of the Scriptures. And it in turn has enriched and blessed me beyond measure. Its emphasis on Jesus and His work—the magnificence of His person as truly, eternally God and yet truly human through the Incarnation, and the glory of His accomplishment as sacrifice, high priest, and coming king—have gripped me, amazed me, inspired me, motivated me, sustained me.

For many years Hebrews had fascinated me. In its language it is the most carefully composed book of the New Testament. Its vocabulary is rich, with words found only here. Its argumentation and logic are powerful, developing step by step in an intricate pattern. Yet throughout most of the twentieth century Hebrews was neglected by scholars. They found its reasoning concerning blood, priests, and sacrifices strange and remote, an echo of a bygone approach to worship. Only Roman Catholic scholars sought to plumb its depths, and they did so from the background of the Mass and the priesthood of their tradition.

Because I wanted to complete my doctoral work at Vanderbilt as rapidly as possible, early on I began to explore possible topics. My major professor, Leander E. Keck, suggested that I consider making a comparative study of the Gospels and the pseudo Gospel written by the pagan Philostratus. In the early years of the church he sought to counter the influence of Christianity by holding up the life and work of Apollonius of Tyana, a miracle worker. But before I even began to learn about this false Gospel, Keck told me that a student at another university had already taken the topic.

No course on Hebrews was offered at Vanderbilt, and in the century-long history of the university no dissertation had focused on this book. I began to wonder: Why not be the first? One day I gingerly broached the possibility with Professor Keck. "Go for it!" he encouraged me. "I would welcome a dissertation on the book of Hebrews." He advised me to go over and over the book itself, listening to its message, trying to understand it on its own terms.

I did so. I read and reread Hebrews in the original Greek. And I discovered something basic, something startlingly simple, but something that scholars had overlooked, although it was staring them in the face. It was there, right at the beginning, in the third verse: "Christ made *purification* for our sins." The human problem—the problem of sin—was being portrayed as defilement, dirt, with Christ's work as a cleansing. Again and again the book played on this theme, with the ninth and tenth chapters spelling out the argument in detail.

How could these basic ideas have been missed? Because interpreters of Hebrews imported into the text the Reformation heritage of justification by faith, which stems from Romans and Galatians. In those books the sin problem has the setting of a law court: we are guilty as charged, but Jesus takes our offenses upon Himself so that we may be acquitted. That is a totally different setting from Hebrews, which can be rightly understood only on its own terms.

As a Seventh-day Adventist I had an advantage over scholars from other backgrounds. My tradition had sensitized me to the concepts of sanctuary, priest, and sacrifice; and the Old Testament book of Leviticus, on which the argument of Hebrews builds, is impregnated with the language of defilement and purification.

I was still in the coursework phase of my doctoral studies, but this breakthrough from Hebrews began to shape my research in other areas. Several of the papers I developed for doctoral seminars fed directly into the dissertation—providentially, I believe. The dissertation, "Defilement and Purgation in the Book of Hebrews," came together after only seven months, in a 400-page draft that required minimal revisions.

For many years I have held strong convictions that the scholarly study of the Scriptures should not be held tight within the circle of academicians. Having been given the privilege of higher study, I feel a burden to make the insights I have gained accessible to the church. Almost all my writing at the popular level has stemmed from this impulse. And so, in Camelot, I set out to share ideas from my dissertation. I wrote the manuscript of a book on Hebrews in the summer of 1977. It worked its way through the publishing process and emerged exactly two years later: *In Absolute Confidence: The Book of Hebrews Speaks to Our Day*.

Subsequently I wrote three other books based on Hebrews. All were requested. One came from John Knox Press for their series summarizing the content of biblical books with preaching suggestions. At the same time I had several scholarly articles on Hebrews accepted by academic journals, including the prestigious *Journal of Biblical Literature*.

With all that I have written on Hebrews, I still think that the first work, *In Absolute Confidence*, was the best and most influential. It circulated widely at the time and—utterly unforeseen by me—would play a critical role in theological developments in the 1980s.

In view of the importance of Hebrews in my life and the church, it seems ironic in retrospect that several people whom I respected highly discouraged me from writing a dissertation on this book. "That's a dangerous book for an Adventist to get into," warned a fellow teacher. And even Edward Heppenstall, under whom I had worked on the M.A. degree at the seminary, worried. "I'm concerned about you, Bill," he said. "Will you still be an Adventist when you get through your dissertation?"

Their concern was based on history. Several Adventist students of Hebrews, including a couple prominent leaders, had parted company with the church as a result of their investigation. So the book had developed a sort of mystique, that it contained ideas that, when probed, might be damaging to Adventist teachings.

I was surprised and disappointed at these cautions, well-meaning as they were. If there is any book of the Bible that is dangerous for Adventists to study, we'd better study it! We are a people of the Book, and only by being open and honest with the Scriptures can we expect the Lord to bless us.

I determined to let the chips fall where they might. I would leave it in the Lord's hands. And my studies led me to greater confidence in the teachings of the Adventist Church, not less. I emerged from my doctoral work a stronger Adventist than when I had entered it.

Today the reservations about Hebrews—that it's a dangerous book for Adventists to study—have disappeared. Perhaps my work helped in the process. In the scholarly world an amazing transformation has taken place: Hebrews has come to the forefront of academic study. And at Vanderbilt two members of my doctoral class also prepared dissertations on this book (the topics quite different from mine).

<hr />

At a Southern Asia get-together on the Andrews University campus, a former student from Vincent Hill School came up to me. "Mr. Johnsson," she exclaimed, "you've ballooned! You must have gained 30 pounds."

Hardly a diplomatic greeting, and an even bigger blow to the ego. I was born skinny, grew up skinny, thought of myself as skinny.

I was used to tiresome comments about having to walk past a spot twice in order to cast a shadow, or that I vanished from view if I turned sideways. And now someone was saying I'd ballooned.

But I had. I had entered my 40s, and the weight had begun to creep up. It was time for me to make some changes in my life.

A notice advertised a free blood pressure clinic in the township, and I showed up. The nurse measured my blood pressure. "H'mmm. One-sixty. You're right on the border of needing medication to lower your blood pressure."

Definitely time for changes.

A new student enrolled in the seminary, an attorney who had joined the Adventist Church. He was a devoted runner and soon organized the Berrien Springers, a running club. For the fall the club planned a 10-mile event—the Thaddeus T. Thudpucker gallop.

Our son, Terry, age 15, entered the run, and I decided to join him. I bought a pair of running shoes and set off down the street. By the time I reached the corner I was out of breath. Bad day, try again. But the next day it was the same story.

Terry ran the 10-miler while I watched from the sidelines. *Next year—next year I'll run in this event,* I vowed.

And I did. During the next year I hit upon a pattern that worked for me. After my seminary classes I'd drive to Lake Michigan and run along its margin. Short distances at first, then farther and farther. I have been running ever since, and it has changed my life. Mind you, I'm not much of an athlete, not a great runner in any sense of the word. I'm *slow*—but I keep plodding along. Even to the 26.2-mile tape of a marathon. I have completed the Marine Corps Marathon 17 times. Twenty-seven years after the Berrien Springs nurse told me I had borderline hypertension, my blood pressure is 120/70, with a resting heartbeat of 45.

More than the numbers, however, running helps me to be a nicer person. I'm still plenty ornery, but not nearly as mean as this tightly wound machine would be without the release that running brings.

Little did I know it then, but the years just ahead would bring stresses and demands that would tax me to the limits of my being. And the habit formed in Camelot would be a major blessing from the Lord to enable me to cope.

———◆———

Throughout the 1970s Adventists wrangled over righteousness by faith. One side emphasized justification, stressing that it was a legal act by which God declared the believer righteous in His sight. The other side stressed sanctification, a growth in holiness in preparation for the second coming of Christ.

Books and articles argued for one position or the other. Preachers used the Sabbath sermon as an occasion to propound their views, often quoting this scholar or that in support. Even the *Adventist Review* and *Ministry* magazines became caught up in the controversy, taking positions at odds with the other.

At the seminary we stayed above the fray, although we followed developments with interest. Then an interesting gentleman from Australia showed up in our midst. Geoffrey Paxton, an Anglican, had become fascinated by what he had heard of the debate in the Adventist Church and decided to make his own investigation. He came to America and visited Adventist colleges, meeting with students and faculty to gauge their understanding of the gospel. When he arrived at the seminary, he requested permission to quiz students in various classes.

He visited one of my classes and handed out copies of a questionnaire he had developed. It consisted of a series of statements to be answered either affirmatively or negatively. As I looked at the questionnaire I figured the students would have difficulty with many of the propositions. Some contained language unfamiliar to them, such as "the doing and dying of Christ." Others reduced complex theological concepts to a simple yes or no.

Paxton went on his way and eventually published a book based on his research, *The Shaking of Adventism*. In it he concluded that the church was in crisis over the gospel: even students at the seminary were confused. The book caused consternation in some circles and further roiled the theological waters.

I strongly disagreed with Paxton's approach. Theology, the study of God and His works, should never be dumbed down to either-or propositions. Very often the answer is not either-or but both-and. For instance: Is God one or three? The simple answer from either-or is wrong: God is both one and three.

Another aspect about Paxton's argument—and one shared by many Adventists, in the debate over righteousness by faith—was confusion in theological terms. He, and many Adventists, used concepts (such as sanctification) as they had been employed by the Protestant Reformers, rather than letting the Scriptures explain their meaning. Thus, in the debate over justification and sanctification, the former was understood as a momentary divine declaration, the latter as something that comes afterward and is ongoing.

My close study of the book of Hebrews had taught me to listen to the text, not read other ideas into it. Now, as I sought to understand how God saves us, I encountered a concept of sanctification sharply at variance with what I was hearing in the current debates. Paul's words in 1 Corinthians 6:11 blew the boat out of the water: "But you were washed, you *were sanctified, you were justified* in the name of the Lord Jesus Christ and by the Spirit of our God." Here Paul listed sanctification as something already accomplished, and positioned it *before* justification.

The Bible uses the verb "to sanctify" and its cognates many times. Simply studying all the occurrences reveals that sanctification can be *past* (as in 1 Cor. 6:11), *present* (those "being sanctified," as in Heb. 2:11), or *future* (sanctification as a goal, as in 1 Thess. 5:23). So, I concluded, the debate over the gospel could be adjudicated only by getting back to the way in which the Scriptures employed the key terms under discussion.

At General Conference headquarters leaders were seeking for a response to *The Shaking of Adventism*. They appealed to the seminary faculty for help. Dean Blincoe requested each teacher to turn in suggestions, asking me to write a critique of the book in light of their comments. My paper became lengthy, not only showing the flaws in Paxton's work, but pointing the way, as I understood it, to resolve the debate among Adventists. The paper was well received at the General Conference.

On January 1, 1979, Elder Neal C. Wilson took office as leader of the world church. One of his first acts was to call for a moratorium on the debate on righteousness by faith. He requested ministers and editors to avoid public discussion of the topic until after he convened a large, representative group to address the key issues. From this meeting would flow one of the most remarkable experiences of my life.

Some 150 people were invited to the council, which met at General Conference headquarters in Takoma Park, Maryland, in October 1979. Administrators, teachers, pastors, editors and writers, and lay members—all were represented. For the first time I saw the Neal Wilson style of leadership in action: deliberate, unhurried, giving all points of view opportunity for a thorough hearing. But I was also puzzled. The two-day meeting, for almost its entirety, consisted of person after person coming to the microphone and making a speech on their understanding of righteousness by faith. There was no discussion back and forth, and minimal analysis of the various views expressed to ascertain their strengths and weaknesses.

Those of us who had come from the seminary expected that the meeting would produce a tangible result, but it became more and more obvious that Wilson had other plans. He simply wanted a complete airing of the topic in its complexity, giving opportunity for all voices in the debate to be heard. The process he had in mind involved the further step of a small, more manageable group to focus discussion and arrive at a conclusion. Thus, toward the close of the meeting, he steered the group in the selection of a committee of 24 who would come together early in the new year.

Three professors from the seminary were included in this group, which was humorously dubbed the "24 elders"—Gerhard Hasel (Old Testament); Fritz Guy (systematic theologian); and myself (New Testament). When the "24 elders" came back to Washington, D.C., in February 1980, Wilson focused attention on the statements that had been developed at the special meetings on righteousness by faith convened during the 1970s. After the "24 elders" discussed the best way to proceed, Wilson recommended that an editorial group should go apart, do its work, and report back the next day to the full committee.

Under the chair's direction, we three from the seminary—Hasel, Guy, and Johnsson—were appointed to the editorial task. We got together and quickly agreed that we should prepare a totally new paper—the ones on hand could not be melded into an effective statement. Since it was already late in the day, we would meet early the next morning, when I hoped to have an outline for us to consider.

My best work has been done in the wee hours of the morning. I rose early and began writing before 4:00 a.m., By the time I met Gerhard and Fritz in the room assigned to us, I had an outline and a good start on the paper. We worked together intensively for a couple of hours, Gerhard giving input and looking up Scripture texts and Ellen G. White quotations, Fritz typing on a battered old machine and making suggestions, and I writing at high speed on a yellow notepad.

When the "24 elders" assembled at 9:30 a.m., we informed them of our progress and requested more time to complete the paper. I have forgotten when we met again—that day became a blur. It would have been before the noon break or just after—but when we did so we had the paper finished, with typed copies for everyone to examine. Titled "The Dynamics of Salvation," the paper dealt with the key issues raised in the debate, but avoided any mention of the polarizing terms *justification* and *sanctification*. It grounded the arguments solidly in Scripture and Christian experience, arguing that in life our standing in Christ can never be separated from our growth in Christ.

Elder Wilson asked me to read the paper aloud, then invited responses from the group. The air was electric as members rose to express their gratitude and appreciation for this paper that seemed to provide a path through the thickets of controversy. One member, a champion of justification, wanted more on the side of his views; another, a proponent of sanctification, pressed for more in that area. The group as a whole, however, urged that the balance struck in the paper not be disturbed.

The committee decided that the draft of "The Dynamics of Salvation" should be published in the *Adventist Review* and copies sent to the large group that had met the previous October. Members of this group, along with *Review* readers, were invited to send in their suggestions. They did so. Many came back and were forwarded to the editing group of Hasel, Guy, and Johnsson. We considered each response and made a few changes to the text. Overall, it remained almost unaltered. We then forwarded the edited statement to the General Conference.

With the circulation of "The Dynamics of Salvation," the debate over righteousness by faith quickly faded away. The 1980s saw heated theological arguments, but the issues that had wracked the church in the prior decade were no longer a part of them.

I look back at "The Dynamics of Salvation" with wonder. I think it is a very fine statement, theologically sound and graciously worded. It is not *my* statement—I do not claim credit for it—but truly the product of the three of us who worked unitedly and intensively through that morning in the little room at church headquarters.

We earnestly sought the Lord's guidance and strength and, as He always does, He came through. We felt His hand over us. I don't want to claim too much—all that we humans do is flawed—but at the risk of being misunderstood, I believe that "The Dynamics of

Salvation" was not *our* statement but *His*.

Some of the "24 elders" could hardly accept that the statement came about de novo that morning. They figured that we brought much of it, or at least the plan of it, with us from the seminary.

But we did not. None of us—Gerhard, Fritz, or I—had been fore-warned of the role we would be called upon to play at the General Conference. I know this for fact: I wrote the original draft, first word till last, and every word originated that same morning. True, I had given the topic of salvation considerable thought in preparing the re-sponse to Paxton's book, and, as had Gerhard and Fritz, inevitably dealt with it in varying degrees in classes in the seminary. What was already in our heads: this is what we brought to the task.

Reflection on "The Dynamics of Salvation" also brings me a note of sadness. We three—Gerhard, Fritz, and I—worked harmo-niously, and the Lord made evident His benediction. But much has changed since that February morning in 1980. Adventist scholars, particularly in the United States, have become divided. They have formed two professional societies that have little to do with each other (though some are members of both societies). In the polarized theological climate that marks our times, it seems inconceivable to younger scholars today that Gerhard Hasel and Fritz Guy in partic-ular could have worked so closely together.

Distrust is the poison of these times; it was not ever thus. Nor, I pray, will it ever be.

------◆------

Seminary faculty members in those days, though overall a very contented bunch, had one beef with the General Conference. They felt bypassed in theological matters. church leaders frequently took up items that had a theological dimension, developing policies with-out inviting input from those most trained for the task. But a notable exception occurred toward the end of my stay in Camelot.

For some time concern had grown at church headquarters over the need to update the Statement of Fundamental Beliefs. The statement in use at that time had some obvious deficiencies— nothing on the Lord's Supper, for instance. It had been written by then *Review* editor F. M. Wilcox in 1931 and had never been formally voted by the church.

The General Conference assigned a committee to revise the fundamental beliefs. They did their work with a view to bringing the recommendations to the General Conference session in Dallas, Texas, in April 1980. Neal Wilson, in his first year as world president, decided to seek input from the church's theologians. He dispatched Richard Hammill, a General Conference vice president, to seek the wisdom of the seminary faculty on the revised statements.

Hammill's meeting with us took an unexpected turn. Quietly but forcefully the seminary faculty pointed to flaws in the revised statements: lack of precision, inadequate wording, and so on. They argued that some new areas—doctrines commonly believed by Seventh-day Adventists, but not included—should be incorporated.

Hammill listened patiently but made clear that his mandate was to share information and seek input of a minor nature. At length, however, he agreed to at least consider alternate wordings for some of the statements, and also the proposed new statements. The faculty quickly parceled out assignments and went to work. My job fell to draft a statement on the Spirit of Prophecy, the one that emerged as number 17 in the 27 fundamental beliefs.

We brought back our work, refining wordings based on the suggestions of our colleagues. Hammill, to his credit, very quickly saw the superiority of the new wordings. Won over, he joined heartily in the endeavor.

Of course, he and the seminary faculty had gone far beyond the mandate Hammill had been given. He called Elder Wilson and shared the news. Wilson made a trip to be with us, spent time discussing the changes (which were major), and agreed with Hammill's evaluation.

So the changed statements and new statements came back to the committee assigned to the fundamental beliefs. They must have been surprised—I would like to have listened in on the discussion—but they accepted them after making a few alterations.

The 27 fundamental beliefs came to the 1980 General Conference session. Discussion lasted for days, as was right. The new statements formed the major item of business at the session.

Although the 27 aren't perfect—what is?—they have served the church well. We are a world church and growing fast; we need a common statement of faith. Not a creed—we have no creed but the Bible—but as a fixed reference point. Because Adventists publish so much and allow writers, editors, and preachers considerable latitude in expressing their ideas, from time to time points of doctrine reflecting a personal bias find their way into print or from the pulpit. It is good at such times to be able to refer to the fundamental beliefs for the definitive statement of what we as a body adhere to.

Permit me to add a footnote to the 27 fundamental beliefs. Twenty-five years later I again became involved in drafting work in this key area. Since 1980 the Adventist Church had grown enormously, reaching out to new peoples and areas previously unentered by Christianity. Many of the men and women we had to deal with, and still seek to contact, live lives dominated by belief in spirits. Still others feel the heavy weight of karma, the accumulated burden of deeds from multiple past existences. For such peoples, as well as others in Western settings who live with a sense of futility and meaninglessness, the 27 have nothing to say to their needs. Out of this mission-driven situation, church leaders saw the need to develop a new fundamental belief.

Three of us worked drafting it—Angel Rodriguez, director of the Biblical Research Institute; Mike Ryan, a vice president of the General Conference heavily involved in mission; and I. The statement went through multiple drafts and multiple committees, with input from church leaders. It was published in the *Adventist Review* and

Ministry, and on the General Conference Web site, with an invitation to all to provide input. At length this statement, "Growing in Christ," number 11 of the now 28 fundamental beliefs, was debated and, after slight modification, voted by delegates to the General Conference session meeting in St. Louis, Missouri, in July 2005.

I had just been appointed associate dean of the seminary when out of the blue I received a call voted by the Review and Herald Publishing Association. It was to join Elder Kenneth H. Wood's staff as an associate editor of the *Adventist Review*.

I saw no light in the call, felt nothing in me urging me to say yes. Neither did Noelene. This one simply wasn't for us.

Elder Wood pursued me diligently, but at length I felt constrained to tell him, "Elder Wood, I am honored by the invitation, but you should look for someone else for the post."

I said to Noelene, "Well, that's one job I'll never be asked to do," and went back to teaching and the new responsibilities as associate dean. Occasionally, however, my mind would wonder, *What if we had said yes?* But the thought did not stick. I had plenty to do, and besides, I was certain that I would never be approached again to connect with the *Adventist Review*.

Two years later we received the sad news of Elder Don Neufeld's sudden death. An associate editor of the *Review*, Neufeld was highly regarded at the seminary for his knowledge of the biblical languages and his careful work on *The Seventh-day Adventist Bible Commentary* and for the church paper.

Shortly after, I had to attend a committee meeting at the General Conference. I sat across the table from Robert Olson, secretary of the White Estate, in C-2, the long room in the old headquarters building in Takoma Park. As we chatted before the committee started, Bob Olson took a small piece of paper, wrote on it, and, eyes twinkling, slipped it facedown across the table.

"If you would say yes," the note read, "I am 99.999 . . . percent certain that the Review and Herald will call you to be an associate editor of the *Review*. But they don't want to have to deal with another no."

The note threw me into temporary confusion. Then the committee got under way, and I became engrossed in the discussion. (We were meeting with Desmond Ford to review the manuscript on his views that he had been requested to write.) After the committee, I returned to the seminary. A month went by, two months. I concluded that the Review and Herald had settled on someone else for the vacant position at the church paper.

Then, one morning, a big surprise! The president of the university walked into my office. "Bill," he said, "you will be getting a series of telephone calls. Elder Wilson's office will call you to set up an appointment with him. Duncan Eva, the Review and Herald board chair, will call you urging you to accept the *Adventist Review's* associate editor post. And Willis Hackett, chair of the Andrews board, will call you urging you to stay at the seminary.

"I think you should meet with Elder Wilson," he went on, "but don't let him persuade you to leave Andrews. Remember, in Washington you will come under heavy pressure to accept."

The telephone rang—Elder Wilson's secretary.

It rang again—Duncan Eva.

And again—Willis Hackett.

Before we knew it, Noelene and I were on a plane headed to Washington, D.C. Elder Ken Wood with his delightful wife, Miriam, met us, acting as our hosts during the visit.

Next day I met with Neal Wilson alone. "Bill," he said, "we need you here. You're doing a good job at the seminary, but we think you should join the *Review*."

As I left his office, I met Elder G. Ralph Thompson, secretary of the General Conference. His eyes sparkling, he looked me in the eye and asked, "Did Elder Wilson bowl you a googly?"

Googly is a cricketing term. It designates a tricky type of delivery, one that looks as though the ball will turn one way, but instead turns the other.

I smiled at Pastor Thompson and did not reply. But my heart was saying, "Yes, he bowled me a googly—and bowled me out!"

Two years earlier the invitation to connect with the *Review* had come out of the blue as a call voted by the Review and Herald board. The second time it came, without vote of any committee, as a telephone call.

Back at the seminary my colleagues were shocked. "You're making a big mistake," opined Gerhard Hasel. He and I worked closely together on the doctoral committee, he as chair, I as secretary. The seminary had just opened up a Th.D. program, and Hasel was determined to set a high standard.

A few of my colleagues disappointed me. They cut me off. They viewed General Conference leadership as the foes of academicians, and by leaving Andrews I had crossed over to the enemy.

So late August 1980 saw us moving to the Washington, D.C., area. Only Noelene and I made the move—Terry and Julie stayed on at Andrews. Apart from the breakup of our closely knit family, we took it on the chin financially. In Berrien Springs, where we had assumed a low-rate mortgage, our monthly mortgage payment was only $148. In the high-priced Washington area market, we had to take out a second mortgage as well as a first mortgage in order to purchase a home. Plus our home in Berrien Springs didn't sell. We locked it up and left it empty. Plus we now had two children in boarding schools, *plus* there was a glut of teachers in the Washington area, so no job open for Noelene. Plus . . .

But we survived. For a couple of years it was a pinch. Each fall we struggled to come up with the cash to enable Terry and Julie to register at Andrews. Looking back, it doesn't seem all that bad, however. We were happy. More than that, we had the assurance that we were where the Lord wanted us to be.

Camelot, where the rain doesn't fall till after sundown and every morning the fog disappears by 8:00 a.m., exists only in the mind. The mind can make its own Camelot, wherever we find ourselves.

We left Camelot. We are still in Camelot.

In the Cockpit

CHAPTER 7

The Little Paper

After coming out of vision, I said to my husband: "I have a message for you. You must begin to print a little paper and send it out to the people. Let it be small at first; but as the people read, they will send you means with which to print, and it will be a success from the first. From this small beginning it was shown to me to be like streams of light that went clear round the world."
—Ellen White, 1848

As editor of the *Adventist Review* I tried hard not to take myself too seriously. The weight of the job is such that it could either crush you or make you insufferably self-important.

The "little paper" plays a role that is unique among denominations, and the editor occupies a responsibility unlike that for any other church organ. Very early in my tenure I began to realize how closely *Review* and church are linked. The church and the *Review*, the *Review* and the church: they are coterminous. In a manner peculiar to our faith communion, paper and church blend, interact, and foster each other.

The *Review* is the leading edge of the church. It seeks to represent the church, to advance the church, and to articulate the church. And as Adventists still seek to be open to present truth, the *Review* challenges the church to the vision splendid, the light on the hill that the Lord of the church holds out for the church.

I took over the editor's desk at a time of fierce controversy. Many Adventists felt angry that they hadn't been told the truth. This difficult period began before my tenure, but it reached its zenith during my first few years. And what especially startled and pained me was this: many letters flowed into the *Review* office, some from ministers and former missionaries, telling us they were canceling their subscription, *not because of the content of the* Review, *but because they were unhappy with the church*. They wanted to make a statement, so they canceled the *Review*.

This sense of speaking for the church, of personifying the church, brings an enormous weight of responsibility. When many Adventists see the *Review* as the church, taking every word very seriously, who can be sufficient to discharge such a commission adequately?

And the job entails far more than editing the church paper. True, that part is central: all else that the editor is called upon to do depends on the paper's regular issues. Only as the *Review* feeds the flock and nourishes the worldwide body will the editor have credibility and inspire confidence in his other roles.

The *Review* editor wears many hats: he travels and speaks widely, across North America and the world; he is a member of the General Conference Executive Committee; he is an invitee with voice and vote to the Administrative Committee of the General Conference, which meets most weeks; he works closely with the printing arm of the church paper, the Review and Herald Publishing Association, and is a member of its board of directors; he is appointed to commissions and task forces, often being asked to prepare papers and critique ideas; and he is a confidant of the General Conference president, to whom he reports and with whom he must work closely, but—for the good of the church—for whom he must not become a mouthpiece.

The *Review* serves a vital role in the communication processes of the church, but it is not part of the General Conference Communication Department. The *Review* is neither the voice of the loyal opposition nor part of the public relations efforts at church headquarters. The paper must keep a distance—not a large one—from administration, so that it can, if the occasion arises, speak with a prophetic voice to the church.

I once formed a friendship with a Mormon who lives in Salt

Lake City. We exchanged letters and e-mails, and he invited me to visit him and his wife. I did so, and he arranged a meeting with some of the leaders of the Latter Day Saints, one of whom oversaw their official publication. The contrast with the *Review* was starling: every issue has to be carefully screened in a process that takes several months. Mormon leadership seeks to ensure that every word of their church paper reflects official thinking.

We Adventists do it differently. I had no reading committee, certainly no censorship group. No one, not even my boss, the General Conference president, told me what to publish or not to publish. Occasionally I asked a couple of leaders to review an article that I figured might be controversial. However, that rarely happened.

The Adventist approach is: select the editor carefully and then trust him to do the job. If the editor fails, replace him.

I like that—from the standpoint of editor, and for what it says about how we function in the Adventist Church.

And the approach has worked. The first issue of the "little paper," initially called *Present Truth*, came off the press in 1849. One hundred thirty-three years later, on December 1, 1982, I took over as editor. I was only the tenth in the line. Considering that some editors served but short periods—J. N. Andrews, A. T. Jones, and W. A. Spicer—the average tenure has been considerable.

The roll call of the nine who preceded me is like walking through a gathering of Adventist "greats": James White, founder of the paper, founder of the church; Uriah Smith, appointed editor at age 23, and in and out of office for the rest of his long life; J. N. Andrews, the church's first scholar and first missionary; A. T. Jones, champion of religious liberty; W. W. Prescott, founder of several colleges; W. A. Spicer, General Conference secretary and later president; F. M. Wilcox, who served for 33 years; F. D. Nichol, towering apologist; and Kenneth H. Wood, who opened up the church paper to give the people a voice and who mentored me for two years.

And now the eleventh editor, Bill Knott, pastor, church historian, graceful writer and speaker. The paper is in good hands.

———◆———

How did I come to be chosen for this heavy responsibility? I do not know. Looking back, it seems surprising. I had worked for the church for 20 years when I joined the *Review* office as an associate editor, but most of the time had been in India. With just five years at the seminary, I was not well known at the General Conference or in North America.

Yet when Noelene and I visited Washington at Elder Wilson's request, we were given a clear signal that more than the associate editor post was being contemplated. I had never met Harold ("Bud") Otis, Jr., president of the Review and Herald, but his first words were "I want you to learn the job and take over as editor of the *Adventist Review*."

And indeed I had a lot to learn. I wasn't trained in journalism; I was ignorant about magazine layout and production; I knew nothing concerning printing.

For the first few months I faced a steep learning curve, as I struggled to become acquainted with a new vocabulary and the unending cycle of a weekly magazine, with four issues at different stages of production always marching in line.

It wasn't easy. I missed the classroom, missed the contact with students and faculty, missed the campus life. I had become part of an environment in which ideas took second place to production and sales. After 20 years of striving for excellence in the classroom and attaining the rank of full professor and associate dean of the seminary, I was back to square one. In the *Review* office those with lesser titles—editorial assistants and assistant editors—knew far more about what was going on than I did.

But the Lord had called—of this Noelene and I were confident. He wanted us at church headquarters so He would see us through the difficult transition. And He did. I stuck it out, gradually feeling more at home, then moving toward mastery of the new work, refusing to listen to the voices inviting me to return to the academic environment.

———•◆•———

As deficient as I was in formal training in journalism, I did bring an essential quality: I love to write. Writing is my creative outlet, the way I express myself; it's my hobby. I have been writing since I was 12, when I won my first prize for writing. I love words; I love poetry; I love fine expression. I enjoy editing, but I love writing.

When I joined the *Review* staff I already had four books in print and maybe 75 articles. By the time I cleaned out the office and shut the door 26 years later, the book tally had grown to 20 and the articles exceeded 1,000.

Right off the bat I felt comfortable with the editorial mode. We frequently surveyed readers to find which parts of the church paper were most popular, and invariably letters to the editor polled number one, with editorials placing second. Over the years I intentionally varied the content of my editorials, seeking for a mix of opinion pieces and devotional material. It gave me great satisfaction to find that my peers in the religious press saw merit in my work. Twice, two years in succession, I was given the top award for editorial writing by the Associated Church Press, which represents about 200 religious journals in the United States and Canada; and several times my writing was recognized under the category of editorial courage.

———•◆•———

It's important that the *Review* editor be able to write well, but two other qualities are even more indispensable. And there is a third, not of the same level, but necessary.

The *Review* editor must be a spiritual person who projects spirituality through life and word. Spirituality is a loose, fuzzy term, but I know of none better to describe the sense of personally knowing God, of being open to His guidance, and to relying on His strength.

For many Adventists the *Review* functions as pastor. Some are shut in, some are isolated, some feel disenfranchised from their local congregation. All these members, and many others, look to the church paper every week for their spiritual food. So the *Review* has to be much more than a vehicle for news of the worldwide church or one to stimulate thought and explore new ideas. The *Review*, in whatever it touches, must impart hope, call to holy living, and lift up Jesus.

The editor's pulpit is very big. He can't see the souls waiting in his congregation, but they are there, hungry to be fed. He must not fail them. Many will write; others will call. He must take time to listen, time to respond.

My work as *Review* editor drove me to my knees as nothing before in my experience. I sought for wisdom, for strength, for patience, for grace. Over the years I saw the Lord come through time and again, pointing the way to go. Staff members became accustomed to hearing me say, "I don't know what we should do, but the Lord does. If we just wait upon Him, He will tell us."

The other quality sine qua non is judgment. You either have it or you don't. If you have it, it can be improved. If you don't have it, no amount of training or experience can supply it.

Judgment means being able to discern what should be printed and what should not be printed. Judgment means being able to foresee the reaction an article or illustration will evoke from readers. Judgment means saying yes or no under pressures of deadlines, with the courage to stop the presses and pull an issue off because of information you've just received.

No one bats 1,000, but the *Review* editor had better have an average much above the usual. And when he "blows" it and something gets into print that with hindsight should not have, he should take it on the chin, even if he was away on a trip when the mistake was made. Adventists don't expect the editor to be perfect, but they expect him to be open and honest. So don't put the blame on someone else. Don't make excuses or give long explanations. A qualified apology is worse than no apology. Tell the people you blew it and that you regret it.

I wanted to open up the *Review*, push the envelope. Sometimes staff members urged me to push it even further. Editorial offices operate like hierarchies, with the buck stopping at the editor's desk. If the editor says "Go ahead," the material goes to press. If he says, "Kill it," it doesn't. Over the years I learned to listen to the little voice in my gut. Early on I occasionally yielded to pleadings from the staff and let material through that my gut warned would cause a problem to the readers. Every time I did so I got bitten and had to try to patch up matters. I learned to trust my gut instincts, and the editors came to accept it without question when I told them my inner voice said no.

All these things I learned on the job. No one taught me, no books told me what to do. Elder Wood had given me tips from time to time, but I had to do it my way. Earnestly seeking the Lord's help to do the work to His glory, I took the road less traveled.

I discovered that there is a third quality the editor needs to cultivate, one not of the same magnitude as spirituality and judgment, but nevertheless necessary if he is to survive in the job, let alone succeed. For want of a better expression, I call this quality *political savvy*.

To be effective in any organization, you have to figure out how the machine works, who are its prime movers and shakers, how to get things done, how to make changes. *Politics* isn't a bad word per se; politics is the art of getting things done. Politics becomes something to be avoided only when unethical means are brought into play, or—in the work of the church—when personal egos and self-advancement govern plans and actions.

I remember well a day very early in my tenure as editor. At that time the General Conference had set up an editorial board with President Neal C. Wilson as chair. That morning I arrived with an agenda bursting with new plans and ideas. Anticipating an enthusiastic response, I presented my great thoughts with vigor, only to see them fall flat. It wasn't that anyone opposed them. It's that no one endorsed them and moved that they be implemented. I went away feeling deflated.

Gradually I began to realize that most people resist new ideas. They have to be brought along to see the light; they don't embrace new plans without a process of education and reflection. Churches are by nature conservative, which brings pluses and minuses—stability, but slowness to embrace change. You have to be patient, do your homework. And you need to work privately and individually with the movers and shakers, presenting but also listening and being ready to modify or even abandon some of your pet plans.

During my 24 years as editor in chief, I spearheaded some major changes. Most of them came well along in my tenure, after I had built up a large treasury of credibility and trust and had become politically savvy.

———◆———

The job of *Review* editor is complicated and grew in complexity on my watch. I interacted with five different "constituencies": the General Conference, the North American Division, the world field, the subscribers, and the Review and Herald Publishing Association. Each was important, and failure to maintain good relations with it would spell disaster for the paper and its editor. The General Conference is the publisher; the General Conference president was my boss. Most subscribers reside in the North American Division, so the editor needs to work closely with the division and union presidents. Subscribers provide the focus of the paper's ministry and the financial base of its operation. Because the *Review* is the *church* paper, not just for North America, the leaders of the world divisions read it carefully, refer to it, reproduce it for their people, and feel a sense of ownership. And from the beginning the Review and Herald, as the printer, has had an intimate relationship with the church paper.

When I assumed office on December 1, 1982, the job title, "editor of the *Adventist Review*," accurately described the work. During the early years I spent most of my time working hands-on and building a first-rate team. But the responsibilities increased. At the time I retired on December 31, 2006, I was not only editor but executive publisher, responsible for the total operation including marketing and finances. And another magazine had been added to the load—the *Adventist World*, of which I was both editor and executive publisher. Plus we had developed an on-line edition of the *Adventist Review* and a magazine for children, *KidsView*, which was inserted once each month into the *Review*. The load had reached a scope and intensity that was almost beyond the limits of my strength and abilities.

Time management has always been important for the *Review* editor; now it became critical. I had to assign priorities, weigh choices among travel, both within North America and the world field, speaking appointments, committees (I was a member of more than 40 General Conference committees); letters and e-mails, several thousand each year; raising the funding for new programs; editorial planning conferences; and staff morale and advancement.

I began my tenure as a hands-on editor. I closed it spending about 25 percent of my time in editing, and some weeks not at all.

———◆———

I never aspired to be the editor of the *Adventist Review*. This post of great responsibility and trust simply came to me—I was called out of the academic environment in which I was happy and thought that I would spend the rest of my life, and placed in a totally different, at first alien, setting, starting over on the learning curve.

Because I hadn't set my eyes on the job, I came to it with much less concern about success or failure than might otherwise have been the case. There was always the classroom to go back to—and from time to time I received overtures about such possibilities.

This sense of freedom that I brought to the office was coupled with strong convictions about integrity. I resolved, come what may, not to sell my soul in order to cling onto the job. I would resign if need be, walk away without any sense of having failed.

Shakespeare's words, found in his play *Hamlet* have been a lodestar of my life for many years:

This above all: *Me Too!!*

To thine own self be true

And it must follow, as the night the day,

Thou canst not then be false to any man.

The years ahead would test me as nothing else in my experience. When you're getting ready to retire for the night and the telephone rings and you hear the voice of the North American Division president (not the current one) saying, "I have all the union presidents on the line with me on a conference call. We have heard that you intend to print an article . . . "—that's pressure!

When the Annual Council is debating a hot issue and someone goes to the microphone and makes a motion that the *Review* should print an article on such and such and you're on your feet reminding the committee that the longstanding practice of the Adventist Church leaves it to the editor to decide what and what not shall be put in the *Review*—that's pressure!

Pressure to compromise came in other forms. Especially during the last 10 years, when we were expanding into new ministry initiatives for the *Review*, we were always looking for ways to fund them. The General Conference office operated on a tight, line-item budget, and as part of church headquarters the *Adventist Review* cost center had to toe the line. There was little money available for new endeavors: we'd have to find the funds for new, ongoing projects. In this situation it was tempting to accept offers from various entities to enter into a business arrangement in return for certain "services." The issue always was whether we would weaken our ability to report fairly and impartially if we accepted the offer.

Over the years I have grown increasingly concerned about the role of money in the church. The church needs money for its global mission (but it needs the Holy Spirit more!), and a large gift can be put to great good. But if the gift comes with strings attached, either overtly or implied, it can mess up the church. It can tie the hands of leaders and hurt the spiritual life of the giver as well.

I was wary of all such schemes, just as I turned down invitations from this institution or that of a free visit, all expenses paid, stay as long as you wish, no obligation to write about us, etc., etc. The way life works is that once you accept a favor, you forfeit the ability to report impartially.

My record isn't simon-pure, but I tried hard to be true to the code of integrity I had set for myself. Life is complicated. Many situations that it throws up aren't straight up or down. What about a board on which you serve that sends you an expensive gift at Christmas? What about the check that comes in the mail after you give an address or present a paper? As a minister, adequately cared for by the church, should you accept these perks?

October 1986. The Soviet Empire will collapse within a few years, but no one will foresee it. The cold war has begun to thaw, and for several years some delegates from beyond the iron curtain have been permitted to attend Annual Council. They say little, but always make a point of publicly proclaiming how great the Soviet Union is, with so much freedom of religion and so on.

It's widely believed that at least one KGB agent is in their midst.

When they return home, they will be interrogated: "Where did you go? What was discussed? What did you say?" The answers they give will determine whether they are permitted to attend the following year.

This year's Annual Council convenes in Rio de Janeiro, Brazil. As is the custom, several days of meetings for the officers of the world church precede the council proper. I do not attend these pre-meetings, but my close friend Bob Nixon does. And he kindly takes along a bundle of the latest *Review* to distribute to the officers.

After careful consideration we are running a two-part series on the Soviet Union and religious freedom. Bert B. Beach, director of the Public Affairs and Religious Liberty Department of the General Conference, has authored both articles. He travels the world, knows conditions in the worldwide church better than almost anyone. The topic is sensitive—we scrutinize any material that concerns countries under Communist rule, lest our people suffer repercussions—but Beach assures us that he has run the articles by the top officers of the General Conference and they have raised no objections.

I arrive in Rio carrying a large parcel of the *Review*—copies of the second issue of the series, just off the press. I feel a healthy pride in our work and want the leaders of the world church to be the first to see it.

Bob Nixon meets me as soon as I come to the hotel. "Bill," he says, "there's big trouble. The delegates from behind the iron curtain are upset by the article on the Soviet Union. They're threatening to pack up and go home."

I am stunned, bewildered. How could I have been blindsided? How could I have failed the church so badly?

The next day the officer group will discuss the matter again, I am told, and I am to be present. It's a painful session. Speaker after speaker stands up and criticizes the article as inaccurate, a slur on Lenin, misleading, and on and on.

I am devastated. Bert Beach is angry.

Bert is no mean scholar—Ph.D. in history from the Sorbonne,

widely read, widely traveled, careful to get the facts straight. And he is also a church statesman, sensitive to political climates and the suffering of our people under repressive governments.

I go to the General Conference president, Neal Wilson, and tell him that if it will help the situation, I will resign. He tells me to stay on the job.

After the litany at last comes to a close, several of those who roundly denounced the article seek me out privately. "Please understand," they plead. "We had to say what we said. . . . Please forgive us."

I do not fault them. If I had been in their shoes, maybe I'd have joined in the chorus of denunciation.

Nor do I fault Elder Wilson and his fellow leaders. Faced with the prospect of years of careful work suddenly crashing over his head, he is faced with a difficult choice. I provide the sacrificial lamb.

In one of his books from that era, Alexander Solzhenitsyn graphically described a speech by a long-winded Soviet leader. One hour, two hours, three hours . . . the boring harangue droned on and on. At last, mercifully, it ceased, and then the rhythmic applause began. One minute, two minutes, three minutes, five minutes, 10 minutes, no one daring to be the first to stop. Eyes were watching, waiting to note down the "offender."

Charade.

I have been caught up in a Soviet charade, Adventist-style.

I go to my room desolate. I look down at the white beach and blue waters. Normally the ocean renews me, but today I just want to get on an airplane and go home.

The pile of *Reviews* that I had carried on the plane sits untouched on the shelf of a closet. I leave them there throughout the council. They are still there when I leave Rio.

My work as *Review* editor brought highs and lows. Rio in 1986 was the lowest of the lows.

Yet the cloud had a silver lining. The next morning at breakfast

Elder Joel Tompkins, president of the Mid-America Union, came up to me. Fixing me with his eye, he said, "Listen, you mustn't feel bad. We all know what that was all about yesterday. And don't even think about resigning, because we in North America won't let you!"

And Rio turns out to be a turning point in my relations with the North America leaders. Relations had been cordial before; now they become warm. These union presidents embrace me as a friend. I am no longer just working for the General Conference; I am one of theirs. They begin to refer to me as *our* Bill Johnsson."

CHAPTER 8

Three Presidents,
Three Bosses

Who knows whether you have come to the kingdom for such a time as this?
—Esther 4:14, NKJV

If the character of an organization is revealed by the type of leaders it selects, the Seventh-day Adventist Church ranks high.

I became editor of the *Adventist Review* on December 1, 1982. For one month the church paper continued to be published by the Review and Herald, as it had from its inception. My boss was the president of the press. But then the publishing house moved from Takoma Park to Hagerstown, Maryland, some 65 miles away. The church decided that as of January 1, 1983, the General Conference would be the publisher, with the editorial staff remaining in the Washington, D.C., area and becoming part of the General Conference family.

Thus, except for the first month, throughout my time as editor I was on the payroll of the General Conference. Reporting directly to the president, I came to know intimately each of the three leaders who guided the church on my watch—Neal C. Wilson, Robert S. Folkenberg, and Jan Paulsen. We worked closely together; I ate at their table; they were so gracious as to eat at ours also. I saw them on the road, representing the church in other countries, meeting heads of state. I observed their struggles with issues and problems of the global Adventist Church. And I developed not only respect for them but admiration.

Without hesitancy or equivocation, I can say that these three—

Wilson, Folkenberg, and Paulsen—led the church well. Not without fault—for who other than Jesus is without fault?—but the Lord empowered and used them for His glory and the advancement of the world work.

These men are very different in personality, their leadership styles likewise. But they share a number of traits.

They literally stand out in a crowd—they are tall men of erect bearing with strong personal presence.

They are world people. They have lived and worked for the church abroad. They know other languages. Neal Wilson spent many years in the Middle East. He understands Arab culture and speaks Arabic. Bob Folkenberg grew up in Cuba, the child of missionaries, speaking Spanish and English. He preaches fluently in both, perhaps a little more so in Spanish. Jan Paulsen, a native of Norway, worked in Ghana and Nigeria. He speaks Norwegian, German, and English.

Wilson and Folkenberg were PKs—sons of Adventist ministers. Paulsen's father, a faithful church member, was a cobbler.

These presidents worked hard. They gave their best for the church. Wilson was often the first person to arrive in the General Conference building, and the janitor would find him still at his desk at 7:00 p.m. When he left for home, he took a briefcase with him— sometimes two—and worked till 11:00 p.m. For many years he got by with only five or six hours of rest a night, managing only three or four hours during the time of Annual Council. I traveled with Folkenberg in Germany, watched as he preached at a large church rally Sabbath morning, met with a youth group in the afternoon, made an international telephone call on an urgent matter, then spoke to another large group of people. All day he gave himself totally, nonstop. When at last we left to return to the hotel, he asked me to take the passenger's seat next to the driver, while he worked nonstop on his computer in the back. Paulsen, like me, rises early—he gets a jump on the day at 3:00, 4:00, 5:00, preparing sermons, focusing on the issues the office will bring to him.

Three presidents, three bosses. Men of fine intellect, high energy. And devoted to the Lord and His people.

All three would have made a mark in the secular world had they not obeyed the Lord's calling to ministry. Wilson might have been a diplomat, holding down a major post in the United States State Department. I could see Folkenberg as the CEO of a large corporation. And Paulsen? President of a prestigious university or heading up an agency of the United Nations.

In the world, men and women of big minds who carry large responsibilities are rewarded with fat salaries. Pastors of megachurches and televangelists live very well. Not so in the work of the Adventist Church. The basic level of compensation from which all salary levels are set is the ordained pastor, who receives an adequate but not handsome monthly paycheck. Conference presidents receive a little more, presidents of unions a bit more, division presidents still more, and the General Conference president—more, but even then only 15 percent above that of the pastor of a local church.

These three, these my bosses, served as Jesus served—not for the money, not for any glory, but to help others.

———◆———

Neal Wilson knew me before I knew him. We first met on the campus of Andrews University shortly after Noelene and I had come from India. I saw him approaching and recognized him, but I knew he would not know who I was. But he walked up to me, put out his hand, and said, "Hello, Bill, how are you?"

Wilson has an extraordinary ability to remember faces, names, and personal details. I have never met anyone else with such recall. This gift, which he must have cultivated, stems from a deep interest in people.

Wilson never met a problem, large or small, that he didn't want to tackle. He didn't shrink from challenges; he welcomed them. As General Conference president he was above all the problem solver.

His leadership style was unhurried, deliberate—focused on one-to-one encounters and committees. Wilson preferred telephone calls to letters, and the calls he made were never short. It might take you weeks to get an appointment, but you received his full attention without worrying about the clock. I have gone to meet him and heard his secretary tell him, "You're running nearly an hour late," but the 15 minutes she allotted me stretched out to 45.

Neal Wilson likewise relished committees—and the Adventist Church runs on committees. The General Conference president, in spite of what some people allege, has no direct, line-item authority. His power is moral and spiritual. And no matter how strongly he may feel about an issue, he cannot demand or command a course of action. Unless the committee authorizes it, nothing happens.

Wilson's mastery of the agenda at the councils of the church became legendary. He studied and prepared for every item, becoming thoroughly versed in the pros and cons, options, nuances, concerns, anxieties. If a major matter came up for consideration, Wilson always took the chair. He usually introduced the item with such words as "Let me make a few remarks . . . " and the delegates smiled. Wilson would weigh out loud all the arguments; he would explore the various aspects; and he did it in such a way that almost everyone, regardless of their opinion on an issue, felt confident that the president agreed with their viewpoint. These "preliminary remarks" always went long, up to one hour or more, depending on the gravity and complexity of the issue at hand.

When Wilson was in the chair, the committee did not break. You had to make your own arrangements to get a drink or visit the restroom. Wilson wouldn't budge all morning, all afternoon, or through a long night session. Committee members humorously remarked to one another that he was like a camel.

At one stage of his presidency Wilson chaired almost all the major boards of the church simultaneously. He wanted to get things done, wanted to make changes, and he set out to accomplish those things by working through the committee system of the church.

It was a centralized, activist style of leadership that accomplished much. The range of concerns through which he guided the Adventist Church—the first major restudy of beliefs in nearly 50 years, the full participation of African-Americans in the life and work of the church, financial crises, doctrinal challenges, the role of the General Conference and its divisions, the role of women—is startling in its scope, variety, and lasting impact.

Inevitably, his unitary approach had a downside. As keen as his mind and as boundless as his energy was, the complexity of a large and growing world church was beyond the ability of any individual to care for on his own. When, as editor of the *Adventist Review*, I was invited to join the Administrative Committee with voice and vote, I was startled to see items on the agenda, listed by date, which had lain untouched for several years.

Some of my colleagues in the General Conference used to complain that they could not get an appointment to meet the president. I did not have that problem. If Wilson was in town, not traveling the world, he would open a spot for me. (This continued to be my experience under the two presidents who came after him.) Wilson took a personal as well as a professional interest in me, perhaps because he had spent years in India and attended Vincent Hill School, perhaps because he had been so closely involved in my leaving the academic world for the *Review* office.

Neal Wilson is a wise man. I valued his counsel as president; I continued to value it after he was no longer president, and not infrequently I sought him out for advice on sensitive issues.

The 1988 Annual Council was scheduled for Nairobi, Kenya. Neal's son, Ted, who was serving in Africa at the time, came up with a plan that would enable his dad to fulfill a lifelong dream—to climb Mount Kilimanjaro. Eventually plans gelled, and six of us— father and son; Delbert Baker, at that time editor of *Message* magazine; two lay members; and I—set off on the grueling five-day trek.

The climb was tough, exhausting, but we all made it. Neal was then 68, one of the oldest to accomplish the feat. I could only admire this man more than ever; this individual who set his mind on a goal and did not turn back until he attained it.

We arrived back from the mountain dirty (we hadn't washed all week), bearded, and smelling bad—and as wildly happy as school-boys who had just won a football game.

But the week wasn't over for Elder Wilson. The next day, Sabbath, he stood and preached to a crowd of thousands who walked from near and far and sat on the ground under the African sun, hardly moving, drinking in every word. If Wilson was tired (I was!), he didn't show it. Nor did he cut the message short!

Two years later Wilson suffered a crushing disappointment at the General Conference session, held that year in Indianapolis, Indiana. On the opening day of the session, he celebrated his seventieth birthday. But, like Moses, his eye was still keen and his step un-abated. He felt that he could—indeed, should—carry on for another term. The Nominating Committee, meeting the next day, decided otherwise—they recommended a change in leadership.

The process is brutal: president today, voted out of office to-morrow. I wish we Adventists could come up with a more com-passionate way of electing our leaders; however, I do not have a plan to suggest. My heart went out to Elder Neal C. Wilson. He did not just pack up and leave. He had to stay on, chairing the ses-sion through sensitive items, keeping the business moving along, although he was now a "lame duck."

He deserved better—much better.

But Wilson refused to allow bitterness to consume him or stint his usefulness. He donned the mantle of elder statesman, giving counsel to Elder Folkenberg and then later Elder Paulsen, keeping open the door of the little office that he retained at church headquarters. All who sought his wise advice were made to feel welcome.

Neal Wilson is still a problem solver.

Robert Stanley Folkenberg blew into the General Conference like a hurricane. His approach to leadership, the polar opposite of Neal Wilson's, rattled the shutters and shook the building.

Bursting with energy and ideas, the new president was impatient for change. At 49 he was the youngest leader of the world church in nearly a century. He brought with him the trappings of his generation: fascination with electronic wizardry, high-tech communication, informality, readiness to try the new.

Folkenberg is a licensed pilot, qualified to fly jet planes. He can handle helicopters also, which demand much more expertise. He scuba-dives. He rides a big motorcycle.

Almost single-handedly the new president jerked the General Conference staff into awareness of the possibilities of the computer age. Laptops replaced secretaries. E-mails became the norm for communication. Longtime administrators and departmental personnel had to retool. The culture changed. Now you saw people wheeling their computer bags behind them as they came to work, then wheeling them out the door at the end of the day.

Folkenberg put high priority on communication. Computer and telephone—these were his tools of trade. Before cell phones became the vogue, he had a telephone that he took with him everywhere, one that reached around the world.

When my telephone rang in the *Review* office and he said, "This is Bob," I never knew where he was. He might be calling from his presidential office one floor above me, or he might be on his way to the airport. Other times he called while in flight, or his voice might originate in London or Nairobi.

He was always on the go. The three presidents I worked with traveled extensively, but Folkenberg more than the others. And wherever he went, computer and telephone went along. He kept up a stream of electronic messages and voice contacts, following developments, trying out new ideas.

And day by day—meaning night by night—he keyed in the electronic diary. He recorded meetings, conversations, impressions, compiling a massive file of information.

Eager to get his message out to the church, he preached widely, wrote much, and did TV interviews and programs. After a few years, his face and byline appeared so frequently that some of us were concerned that he risked overexposure, and told him so.

As new leader of the church, Folkenberg wanted a medium through which he could speak to the Adventist family everywhere. He discovered that nothing was available that seemed to meet his needs. In all the communication processes and publications that the church ran, gatekeepers stood in the way. Eventually he figured that the *Adventist Review* network, incomplete though it was, afforded the best print venue for him to get his ideas out. Thus, he and I developed a close working relationship. Our cooperative efforts went beyond material for publication, and at his request I accompanied him on several trips abroad—to Mexico, to the Soviet Union, to Germany, to Bangladesh, to Southeast Asia.

Folkenberg also saw the possibilities of communication via satellite and pushed for the development of a global network. He wanted the church to sharpen its image to the world, and on his watch an official logo for the global church was designed and put in place, while Adventists as a people of *hope* became the official emphasis in communication.

While Neal Wilson reveled in the committee process, Folkenberg suffered it. He moved through agendas as rapidly as possible, completing the business of councils often well ahead of schedule. He wanted action. He became impatient with the often cumbersome procedures of the General Conference with its multitudinous committees. Folkenberg was a maverick.

Above all else, he was the president of change. He occasionally referred to "leadership by destabilization"—upsetting the applecart in order to move the organization off dead center. And he practiced it, making a series of radical (or radical-sounding) statements at key venues. He shook up those who heard him speak or heard his ideas secondhand—people in Adventist health care, publishing, education, and so on.

I was present when he dropped one of his bombshells. The occasion: celebrations at the William Miller farm in Low Hampton, New York, marking the 150th anniversary of October 22, 1844. Elder Folkenberg was the featured speaker, and uplinked to a satellite and broadcast live. My part was to introduce the event to the satellite audience; then I went into the satellite truck and watched the program as it went out. Everything had been timed to the minute, including the message that the president was delivering. Suddenly the scene in the truck broke into consternation—the elder had departed from his script! He had launched into concerns about Adventist colleges and teachers who were derelict in their duties. After several pointed sentences, he picked up the script where he had broken off.

The following Monday, back at the General Conference, he joined Noelene and me at our table in the cafeteria. As we reviewed the events of the previous Sabbath, he told us that he had carefully chosen that occasion to share his convictions on education to as large an audience as possible.

It was a high-risk strategy, but one that matched Folkenberg's personality and practice. He had piloted airplanes in dangerous situations and seen the Lord deliver him, and he had confidence that the same Lord would be with him as he piloted the world church.

Those who worked closely with Elder Folkenberg found themselves drawn into the vortex of his high-energy activity. I was one of those. Before long my life, already running at high speed, was racketed up another notch.

His secretary would call and say that he wanted to see me—right now. I'd go to his office, and he would share a new idea that he'd been working on. After a brief testing of my reaction, he'd say, "Now this is what I want you to do . . ." It was the same for all of us in whom the elder placed confidence. He would dream up ideas and plans, then leave them with others to figure out how to implement them.

Usually within a day or two he would call me again. "How's the assignment coming along?" he'd ask. No matter that my days already were full with *Review* work—the president expected me to give his project priority. It was flattering, and it was killing.

In both the manner of his coming to the office and his leaving it, the Folkenberg presidency was highly unusual. At the 1990 Indianapolis General Conference session, after the Nominating Committee had decided to made a change, they spent several hours discussing candidates. Late in the day, with delegates restless from the long wait and concerned about the approaching Sabbath, the choice fell, not to a vice president of the General Conference, not to one of the leaders of the world field, not even to a union president—but to a leader at the conference level. Robert Folkenberg, president of the Carolina Conference, had held leadership posts in Inter-America, and he had been selected as chair of the same Nominating Committee that eventually recommended his name to the body as the new president of the world church. It was an outcome almost no one had foreseen.

Folkenberg was catapulted into the presidency; he also left it abruptly. That departure, enveloped in sadness and tension, calls for a chapter in its own right (See chapter 12, "The Swelling of Jordan").

———◆———

Although people who don't know Jan Paulsen well usually address him as "Dr. Paulsen" or "Elder Paulsen," he prefers to be known as Pastor Paulsen. His leadership and life reflect this wish. Above all else that he brings to the office, he is the pastor president.

The Paulsen touch—caring, personal, warm—became apparent from day one of his presidency. He was elected during the afternoon of March 1, 1999, after a morning of high drama and tension that climaxed in the full General Conference Executive Committee's accepting the resignation of President Robert Folkenberg. The next day the church's new leader invited the General Conference family to assemble in the chapel for a get-acquainted meeting.

Every seat was filled as Jan Paulsen, accompanied by his wife, Kari, simply walked out onto the platform. No one else—no one to make a speech or introduce them. No fanfare. They just came before the headquarters staff on their own.

After a few words of welcome, Pastor Paulsen invited Kari to speak first. Apologizing for her lack of experience in public speaking, Kari gave a scintillating 20- to 25-minute talk. Delivered wholly without notes, it was wise, funny, and down-to-earth. It held the audience spellbound. Her husband followed—which in itself was a tough act—and built on the rapport Kari already established.

It had been a down time at General Conference headquarters. During the previous several years the mood of downsizing had cast an air of gloom over the complex. Some workers, even though elected by the world church, had lost their jobs to the ax of greater efficiency. Others were apprehensive about their future. And for the past two months waves of uncertainty had roiled through the halls, as the presidency itself went through a period of crisis.

As the staff filed out of the chapel that morning, the change in spirits was palpable. They had heard words of calm and reassurance from two people who were *real*—comfortable with each other and comfortable enough simply to come before the people without show or buildup.

Acting on his expressed wish to get better acquainted, Paulsen began to visit the various staff in their offices. Without appointment or notice, he just showed up at the door and sat down to chat. No agenda, certainly no sense of evaluation—just getting to know the staff better. No one could remember anything like that ever happening before, and it worked wonders for morale.

The new president was before all else pastor—this was his priority.

Paulsen brought the same calm and graciousness to the General Conference committee system. Never ruffled, he kept members to the agenda without pushing or cajoling. If the vote on an item went the other way, he simply accepted it and moved on. He respected the committee process, believing that if the vote had been a mistake, the Lord would handle it in His way.

This strong sense of the Lord's superintendence over the church was, and is, a hallmark of the Paulsen era. He projected calm and trust because he was calm and trusting. The demands of the office were enormous and many problems seemingly intractable, but Paulsen's hand was always firm on the wheel. "Steady as she goes," I heard him say, and that is what he practiced.

As the church grew ever faster, passing a million new members annually, Paulsen was content to turn over complex management to the national leaders who were on the ground. He refused to micromanage. Instead, he trusted elected leaders and empowered them.

Paulsen had a deep respect for the myriad cultures of the global Adventist Church. He tried to uphold the dignity of all members of the family, and affirmed them in their culture. It was his idea that we publish a large, undated issue of the *Adventist Review* highlighting the marvelous diversity of Adventism, through well-chosen words, but chiefly through photographs. He also suggested the title: "A Tapestry of Adventism." It took us months to secure top-quality pictures from around the globe and then to find choice, short essays. Assistant editor Kim Maran poured her considerable creative powers into the issue and brought it to fruition. It was one of the banner issues of the *Review* on my watch.

Because doctrine is important to Adventists, General Conference presidents work hard to ensure that no departure from the faith will occur during their term. In this respect Paulsen had a considerable advantage over the two men who preceded him. They were qualified theologically but not in depth. Paulsen, by academic preparation and teaching, is a top-drawer theologian. Unlike Wilson and Folkenberg, he did not feel the need to rely heavily on the counsel of others in theological matters. This in turn contributed to the aura of serenity that surrounded him.

Paulsen worked hard on the messages he brought to the people. I heard him preach many times, but not once did I find him repeating material. His ideas invariably were new, fresh, proceeding out of the Word. They were his own, hammered on the anvil of prayer and study in the wee hours of the morning. Communication took giant strides forward under his encouragement—notably the global Hope Channel and the *Adventist World*—but I think that it was his sermons, more than any other feature, that nurtured the church and helped to keep it united.

One Tuesday the members of the Administrative Committee gathered together as usual at 9:00 a.m. As the meeting was about to begin, someone mentioned that an aircraft had just crashed into the World Trade Center in New York City. We got into the business at hand, but before long a messenger came to the door to report that the second tower had been struck by an airplane. By now it was impossible to concentrate on the agenda, and as we struggled to comprehend what was happening, we heard that the Pentagon, about 15 miles away, had also been attacked. Soon yet another message stated—falsely—that the State Department had been hit.

The committee broke up in confusion, members rushing to join the others in the complex who had clustered around TV sets. Fear and consternation gripped the building: Was the United States being invaded? Were we safe? What should we do?

Then a message came over the public-address system for everyone to assemble in the chapel. The anxious employees crowded inside, and Pastor Paulsen strode to the podium, Bible in hand. He shared with the people the facts about the attack, as they were known at the time, then read words of hope and promises of the Lord's protection. He did not speak for long, but his words conveyed calm, trust, and caring. If anyone needed personal help, he said, chaplaincy counseling would be made available. If anyone felt they needed to go home, that would be fine.

Once again the pastor president had ministered to his flock nearest at hand.

———————◆◆◆———————

Three presidents, so different in backgrounds and abilities.

Three presidents, so unlike one another in the way they led the world Adventist Church—problem solver, change agent, pastor.

Each—in the Lord's providence, I believe—was right for the time. Neal Wilson could encompass the global church, but he would be the last General Conference president for whom that might be a possibility. The church was changing, growing very rapidly. It would be beyond any one president's powers, no matter how great they were.

Over the years the church had become institutionalized, the General Conference bureaucratic. Rethinking was needed; change was needed. It would take a hurricane to blow away the old. Bob Folkenberg was that hurricane.

After him, the church needed more than ever a calm, steady hand on the wheel; a hand that understood and loved the amazing, beautiful tapestry of Adventism; and a hand that would continually point the people to look upward in trust and hope. Jan Paulsen was that hand.

Oh, what a privilege was mine—to have known and served with giants!

CHAPTER 9

FDR

The elevator to success is out of order.
You'll have to use the stairs . . . one step at a time.
—Joe Girard

During the early 1980s the Seventh-day Adventist Church was wracked by a series of controversies. Commonly dubbed "FDR", they centered in three Adventists: theologian and teacher Desmond Ford, investor Donald Davenport, and church pastor Walter Rea.

Ford, an Australian, had considerable influence in the South Pacific and North America. A charismatic person, Ford traveled widely and was in demand as a public speaker. He also wrote frequently for Adventist journals, especially *Ministry*. His favorite topic was the prophecies of Daniel, especially Daniel 8:14 and 9:24-27. In 1978 his commentary on Daniel was published by Southern Publishing Association.

In both oral and written presentations, Ford followed a debating style that led him to set up strong contrasts between his viewpoint and those of others. A longtime teacher at Avondale College, he developed a strong following among ministers and lay members. Some, however, strongly opposed his positions, especially his emphasis on justification. As controversy grew, church leaders arranged for him to move to Pacific Union College, where he taught as a visiting professor. The controversy did not cease, however.

Matters boiled over on October 27, 1979. In the course of a Sabbath afternoon address, Ford delivered a broadside against the traditional Adventist understanding of Daniel, with the interpretation of the 2300-days prophecy and the associated 1844 date a particular point of attack. His remarks, which were audiotaped, spread rapidly and caused a firestorm. Ford was put on leave and asked to write out his positions in preparation for a major conference on the Sanctuary that would be convened in 1980.

Davenport, a medical doctor, offered high returns on investments, and both individuals and Adventist entities placed funds with him. Eventually his scheme collapsed, causing many to lose their investments and leaving them embittered. In the wake of the fiasco, the General Conference appointed a commission chaired by treasurer Lance Butler to probe the matter and to decide if any church employees should be disciplined for their part in the failed scheme.

Over the course of several years Walter Rea had become increasingly involved in researching Ellen White's apparent literary borrowing in preparing her books. Charging that the church had covered up the real story behind her writings, Rea agitated that church leaders face the force of the data he had uncovered. In response, the General Conference set up a blue-ribbon committee to meet with Rea and consider the data he had assembled. The meeting took place in January 1980 at Glendale Hospital in California.

Rea, however, was not satisfied with the committee's conclusions. He subsequently published his findings in *The White Lie*, a negative work that came off the press in 1982.

FDR—Ford, Davenport, Rea—delivered triple blows in quick succession. Many Adventist were affected in different ways. For some, the theological dispute and the perceived ill-treatment of Desmond Ford was the main source of complaint. Others felt the sting of financial losses and blamed church leaders for not warning them sufficiently of the risks. And still others, devoted to Ellen White and her writings, felt the ground swept away from under them by material from Walter Rea that cast doubt on the integrity of her work.

I came to Washington in 1980, when these three blows had just begun to be felt. I took over as editor December 1, 1982, when the controversy had reached fever pitch. The years immediately ahead would be the most turbulent and difficult in my experience. Forces seemed ready to tear the church apart. For many, the in thing was to put down the church, its standards, its leaders, and Ellen White. If it was Adventist, it was bad or stupid, something to joke about. It was as though the spirit of the 1960s that convulsed American society had sprung up 20 years later among Seventh-day Adventists.

At the *Adventist Review* we were in the eye of the storm. During those years many Adventists, feeling disillusioned, frustrated, or just plain angry, vented their passion on the *Review*. I got many long, harsh letters, often with instructions to cancel the subscription. Often I found it hard to determine whether the writer was coming from the "left" or from the "right"—the attitude and spirit were identical from both camps.

I spent a lot of time on the road during those years. My study and writing on the book of Hebrews put me in the forefront of the theological debate, and I was asked to speak at many workers' meetings and other church gatherings. I always allowed plenty of time for questions and answers, and sometimes the sessions would drag on for hours. A typical weekend started with a Friday evening vespers, took in the Sabbath morning preaching service, and gave over the rest of the Sabbath to frank and sometimes heated, bitter questions. I would return home utterly drained. It wasn't easy to be the target of the generalized rage of certain church members simply because I came from the General Conference.

Thankfully, the anger slowly subsided. Many ministers and members, weary of argument, tuned out theological discussion. And of course, many no longer were with us—they had dropped out. Some of them had been my students at the seminary. In the South Pacific the church lost most of the ministers and teachers of that generation.

How do you get through times like that? One day at a time, step by plodding step. You do your best, give the work everything you've got, and leave it with the Lord. You comfort yourself with the promise that Christ is the Lord of the church and He will bring her through to calmer waters.

FDR—I was not equally involved with all three, but I was involved. I would find myself tested as never before in my experience.

———◆———

I have known Desmond Ford for many years, but I do not understand him. He is a complex person who defies easy analysis. He has been shaped by personal factors and the Australian environment, which at times is wanting in compassion and graceful discourse.

Ford has a razor-keen mind that makes him formidable in debate. He is able to assemble materials from a wide range of sources and rattle off, in machine-gun fashion, quotations from the Scriptures, Ellen White's writings, or others. He is intense, focused.

We first met at Avondale College as fellow students. I was working on my ministerial studies while he had returned from the field to complete a bachelor's degree, which had not been offered when he first attended the college. Over the years we had some acquaintance. When our family went back to Australia on furloughs from India, I would look him up at Avondale, where he was then teaching. Once I found him sick as a dog, unable to get off his bed. He had left instructions that he didn't want to meet with anyone except me.

When you spent time with Des, it was most often on foot. "Let's walk as we talk," he'd say, and he would stride out toward the mountains. You found yourself struggling to keep up, huffing and puffing and attempting to get a word in.

Des does much better at talking than listening. His mind races ahead, pausing only slightly over what he has heard, always moving on to what he will say next.

Some Adventists have raised Ford to heroic dimensions. For others he invokes only negative feelings: he is a false teacher who has led many astray. I can agree with neither view. To me he is a tragic figure whose very large talents might have been put to use in defending the Seventh-day Adventist Church instead of attacking it.

Ford spent so much time on the problems of interpretation of Daniel 8:14 and 9:24-27 that eventually they consumed him. In the New Testament the book of Hebrews became important for him because of its links with the sanctuary doctrine. In Hebrews, he claimed, we find the counterpart of Leviticus in the Old Testament, and the Adventist teaching about the pre-Advent judgment must be found here if it is true. But, Ford argued, Hebrews does not set out this teaching. Rather, it focuses on the cross as the antitype of the Day of Atonement. Thus, Des concludes, the Adventist understanding of 1844 and the "investigative judgment" is falsified by the Book of Hebrews.

Seven years before Ford brought the house down with his Sabbath afternoon presentation, I had carefully worked through the book of Hebrews in my doctoral dissertation, the heart of which sets out an exegesis of Hebrews 9:1-10:18. Five years later I had prepared a popular version of the dissertation in a book published under the title *In Absolute Confidence*. This work, written in 1977, came off the press (Southern Publishing Association) in the summer of 1979, several months before Ford's address at Pacific Union College.

Later some people thought I had written the book to counter Ford. A few suggested that it was clever of "the brethren" to oppose one Aussie's ideas with those of another Aussie. I told them: "Listen, *In Absolute Confidence* wasn't written to counter Ford. Its ideas came from my doctoral dissertation, written seven years earlier. And the book itself was already in print before Ford gave his famous presentation."

My work on Hebrews, embodied in the dissertation and *In Absolute Confidence* (and in three subsequent books on Hebrews), differed at crucial points from Ford in the interpretation of Hebrews 9:1-10:18. Ford sees the Day of Atonement as the hermeneutical key to understanding the close-knit argument. I do not. The comparison and contrast is not the Day of Atonement against Calvary. It is the entire scheme of sacrifices, of which the Day of Atonement is a major part, over against Christ's once-for-all sacrifice of Himself on the cross. The difference in interpretation becomes critical for Adventist theology.

By nature and inclination I am a reconciler, not a debater. My work on Hebrews, however, threw me into the theological maelstrom that engulfed the early 1980s. Feelings in meetings often ran high, as ministers and lay members struggled to decide whether to stay with the church or sever their connection. One memorable weekend involved the Paradise church in California, where the congregation was convulsed over Ford's teachings. The associate pastor, a young man who had been one of my students at the seminary, had taken away about 120 members and formed a new group that met separately. I spoke to the congregation Friday evening and Sabbath morning, then took questions for several hours in the afternoon. The young pastor came to the afternoon meeting with some of his members, and that evening I continued the discussion at his home.

A few days later I received a long letter at the office. The writer, a Bible worker, told me she had attended the meetings on Sabbath and had a series of questions for me. "If you can't give me answers," she warned, "I am through with this church." I looked at her list and prayed for wisdom and love in framing a reply. All her questions stemmed from the book of Hebrews and the understanding of the Day of Atonement in its argumentation. I worked through all her concerns and mailed off the letter. After some time I heard back from her. "Praise God," she wrote. "I thought I would have to leave the Adventist Church after so many years, but you have given me sufficient answers to my questions. Thank you!"

I wish I could report a similar result for Desmond Ford. I tried hard, but to no avail. After his controversial presentation at Pacific Union College, Ford was placed on leave and instructed to write out his views. A committee, of which I was a member, was appointed to review his manuscript and critique it. In due course a major conference would be convened to consider and discuss his ideas.

Ford plowed ahead, preparing a study of the sanctuary doctrine that grew to about 1,000 pages. The committee met with him three times, evaluating the manuscript as it proceeded. We had open, frank discussions, but they proved to have been largely for naught. The final draft of his views embodied only cosmetic alterations. None of the major concerns raised in the committee were incorporated. I felt let down, as did the other members.

Questions concerning the sanctuary and 1844 had arisen periodically through the life of the Seventh-day Adventist Church. Some Bible teachers no longer felt clear in presenting the traditional position, and many preachers avoided the topic. Ford had put his finger on a sensitive spot, and the newly elected General Conference president decided that the time had come for a major theological conference to consider this unique but increasingly neglected Adventist doctrine.

Wilson decided to call together a large international group—more than 100—to consider the questions raised by Ford. Ford, although present, was not to be on trial, only his ideas. And so in August 1980 the Glacier View Ranch, a church-owned facility more than 9,000 feet above sea level in the Rocky Mountains, became the venue of an historic conference for the Adventist Church.

Glacier View, as the event soon came to be known, generated widespread interest at the time and in subsequent years. Just what happened there has been analyzed, debated, and disputed. Some who did not attend felt confident to argue about it as though they had been present.

At Elder Ken Wood's request, I reported on the conference for the *Adventist Review*. Although still technically part of the seminary faculty, I was on call to the *Review*, and immediately after Glacier View, Noelene and I moved to the Washington area.

The three of us who had worked on "The Dynamics of Salvation"—Hasel, Guy, and I—again were co-opted to prepare a consensus statement. Basing our report on the findings handed in by discussion groups and materials and speeches given at plenary sessions, we reaffirmed the church's sanctuary doctrine while pointing out areas that needed further study. The report was discussed by the body and voted overwhelmingly. Desmond Ford expressed himself in agreement with the report.

Another document suddenly made its appearance on the final Friday morning of the Glacier View conference. Presented orally, and never discussed or voted, it set out a critique of Ford's positions as expressed in his long study prepared for the conference. This document was given prominence in subsequent discussions of Glacier View.

Unlike impressions of Glacier View in subsequent discussions about the event, the time spent together was harmonious, if intense. Desmond Ford himself was at the center of moments of high drama. Initially the conference organizers had intended that he should not address the gathering, but they yielded at length to requests from delegates who had never seen or heard Ford. In a moving encounter, Edward Heppenstall, who was Ford's mentor, made a long public appeal to Ford to consider where his views were taking him. Then President Neal C. Wilson put himself on the line, urging Ford to put his ideas "in his pocket" and not agitate them if the church did not see light in then. The assembled delegates held their breaths, wondering if Ford would accept the counsel of the world leader. Instead, Ford gave a brief reply that he would think about it, and strode from the room.

It was a moment charged with destiny. As we left the meeting, I fell in with an Andrews University officer. "This is an historic moment," he said. "It is very sad." Later in the week Ford apologized for his curt response and adopted a more conciliatory tone. But when I took a long walk with him on Sabbath afternoon, he began weighing the pros and cons of leaving the Adventist ministry. Some people very close to him were telling him that he wasn't as appreciated as he should be, and that he might as well sever the ties. Along with some others I urged him to pull back from taking such a step.

Thus, the Glacier View conference proper came to a close on an upbeat note. Immediately afterward however, everything fell apart. The leaders who had come from the South Pacific felt they needed to receive assurances from Ford about what he intended to teach and preach when he returned to Australia. I was not part of that meeting and do not know all that happened or what options were presented to him. Later, however, I returned to the lobby of the ranch and found Des's wife in a stage of agitation. She had been telephoning friends in Australia with word that Ford was being forced out of the ministry.

I was dumbstruck, bewildered by the sudden course of events. Along with others I had worked hard throughout the week trying to keep the conference united. Suddenly all the effort seemed to have been for naught.

Later the events of that meeting with Ford became rolled into the Glacier View conference itself, although the meeting had officially closed at Friday noon. The negative perception that many came to hold about Glacier View was actually derived from the meeting of South Pacific Division leaders with Ford.

After Glacier View Elder Duncan Eva, a General Conference vice president, worked hard in trying to save Desmond Ford for the Adventist ministry. He kept in contact with him for years, trying to find a way for Des to be reintegrated into the church's working force. A couple years after Glacier View Elder Eva arranged for a few of us to meet with Ford to discuss possibilities. Nothing came of the meeting, however.

I look back on this period of my life with a mixture of strong feelings. Some of those who dealt with Ford subsequently demonized him; I could not then, and I cannot now. At the same time, Desmond was the despair of many of us who loved him and who were pained to observe the trajectory of his life and work. We found him to be a hard person to help. He had a stubbornness about him in theological matters: he was quite sure—too sure—that his views were correct. As powerful as his theology was in stressing the individuality of our standing before God, justification, it was correspondingly weak in the corporate aspect, the doctrine of the church. Thus, I don't think that Des ever grasped the negative fallout from his ideas and the way he propagated them—the loss of personal faith and loss of ministers and teachers. His ecclesiology, the doctrine of the church, is lamentably weak.

Those of us who worked closely with Ford as he prepared his 1,000-page study tried to disabuse him of his negative view of the pre-Adventist judgment. He could only see it as a teaching that destroyed assurance of salvation, and therefore, it was wrong and should be jettisoned. We saw it otherwise but could not get through to him. It was this aspect of theology, I believe, that impelled Desmond Ford to radically recast his views of 1844 and the judgment.

I never met Dr. Donald Davenport, a physician, nor did I ever have any dealings with him. However, the controversy surrounding his name brought me to a critical moment of decision very early in my tenure as editor.

For several years Davenport, who contracted with the United States government to build post offices, offered high returns to those who invested funds with him. Several church entities, including conference and unions, took up his offer and received very attractive payments. As the word spread, various individuals, including General Conference president Robert Pierson, placed personal funds with Davenport. Although church officials did not actively canvass support for the scheme, the fact that church organizations and leaders had confidence in Davenport's investments was sufficient to convince others that the scheme was safe.

But the old adage "high returns, high risk" holds true whether or not the person running a scheme is an Adventist, whether or not church entities and the church president have invested with him. After a few years the Davenport investment program collapsed, as it was certain to do. As the news broke and the extent of the losses began to be known, leaders faced not only loss of money but loss of confidence on the part of laity. Some early estimates put the tag at $60 to $70 million; individuals suddenly found that their life savings, which they thought had been placed in a sound investment, were gone.

The scandal could not have broken at a worse time. Already Glacier View and the Ford controversy had led to anger, suspicion, and accusations. Walter Rea had published *The White Lie*, a vitriolic attack on Ellen White and her writings. And now a financial nightmare: critics of church leaders made them out to be both greedy and incompetent.

Although former president Robert Pierson had invested with Davenport, the General Conference as such had not. It set up a commission headed by General Conference treasurer Lance Butler to make a thorough investigation and to determine which, if any, church officials were culpable.

All this happened in the years leading up to my taking over the editor's desk. The Butler commission completed its work and named various church leaders who, it recommended, should be subject to church discipline for delinquency of duty in the scandal. Further, these individuals were to be specifically identified in the *Adventist Review*.

I had been in office only a couple of months as matters moved to a climax. On one occasion I attended a committee at Loma Linda in southern California. A reporter tracked me down and called to ask if the *Review* intended to print the names of the Davenport "offenders," as the commission had recommended. Without hesitation I told the reporter that we planned to print the names.

Up to this point, engrossed with the new responsibilities, I had given little thought to the matter. Now, however, it began to weigh upon me. To single out those who had erred—was this the role of the church paper? Print is unforgiving. What is written is written forever. Was this something that I should permit to happen on watch?

I became more and more troubled. Increasingly I felt that such publication of offenders was inappropriate, out of keeping with the storied history of the *Review*. The *Review* is about hope, not condemnation. But how could I, newly come to office, oppose what church leadership at highest levels thought should be done?

At length, after weeks of wrestling, my mind was clear. I would go to Elder Wilson and tell him—reluctantly—that if he wanted the Davenport names printed in the *Review*, he would have to find a new editor to do it. I would quit rather than be responsible for such an action.

With speech at the ready, I met with Neal Wilson. Before I had a chance to get into my prepared words, however, he said, "Bill, I've been thinking about those names we were going to print in the *Review*. I don't think we should go ahead." I could scarcely believe my ears. Quickly I told the elder that I had reached the identical conclusion.

The names were never printed. Some people at the General Conference, including a few of my staff, didn't like the reversal. But printing the names would have been a terrible mistake, as events not long after showed. Upon further investigation—as those accused were given opportunity to defend themselves—the commission modified the list, deleting some names. What a colossal blunder to have printed the initial list, as was first planned! Even though a correction would later have been issued, the words in cold, hard type would have been there forever, a blot on the pages of the church's journal.

For me the experience was a trial by fire. Totally unanticipated, it forced me to critically examine my role in leading the *Review*. It steeled my resolve to be true to myself and to the Lord whatever the cost—even to resigning the editor's post.

The dust from the Davenport fiasco gradually settled. When all the accounting was over and insurance payments were made, the losses came out way less than first indicated—less than $10 million, instead of the $60 to $70 million figure that had been bandied about. Offsetting these losses were the several years of high returns that investors had received. Nevertheless, the Davenport investments left a bad taste in the mouths of Adventists for many years afterward. They contributed heavily to the crisis of confidence that shook the church in the 1980s.

———◆———

The third member in the FDR trilogy, Walter Rea, was a fascinating character. He wrote me frequently, usually enclosing many pages of material that, he asserted, showed Ellen White's literary borrowings from a variety of sources. I met him in person at Glendale Hospital in California in January 1980 when I was asked to serve on the blue-ribbon committee set up by the General Conference to give Rea a hearing.

The meeting with Walter Rea lasted two days. For the first day Rea was given the floor, and he presented a great deal of data. Much of it was new to those of us around the table. Some of the data was immediately convincing in showing parallels between Ellen White's writings and the work of others, while some was more problematic. Obviously Rea had devoted many hours of research to the project.

During the second day we asked Rea to listen rather than present, as the committee probed and analyzed the evidence Rea had given them. Some strong exchanges marked the discussion, however. Two of us around the table were scholars of the New Testament—Fred Veltman, of Pacific Union College, and myself. In our doctoral preparation we had been exposed to the literary problems of the Synoptic Gospels—Matthew, Mark, and Luke. In places these biblical texts show word-for-word correspondence, as well as surprising differences elsewhere. Unless one believes that the Holy Spirit dictated the Gospels to the writers, someone clearly is "borrowing" from the work of another.

When Fred and I pointed this out to Rea, he became incensed. "Why do you want to destroy the Bible to save Ellen White?" he charged. To us it was a strange response—we weren't out to destroy the Bible or Ellen White, but merely showing that the Scriptures themselves gave evidence of literary "borrowing" similar to Ellen's writings—a response that revealed a great deal about Water Rea's relation to the data he had uncovered.

The committee concluded that, while Rea had gathered significant material that warranted further study, he was not the person to undertake the work. In time the General Conference, acting on the committee's recommendation, assigned Fred Veltman to the task. He embarked on a long, thorough study of *The Desire of Ages*. Although he was able to demonstrate convincingly that Ellen White drew upon several other literary sources in preparing her classic work, he also established that her use of other writers did not diminish the individual, creative effort that made the book all that it is.

Rea was not satisfied with the work of the committee and the General Conference's response to his research. He went ahead and published his own findings in *The White Lie*.

Controversial though Rea was and threatening to the faith of many (as his research proved), he prodded the Adventist Church to further efforts to understand the prophetic gift as manifested in the life and work of Ellen White. The church as a whole slowly moved away from a verbal (dictation) view of her writings, although that had never been the official position and Ellen herself had denied it. In addition, the Ellen G. White Estate through its board of trustees adopted a series of policies that opened up all her writings, published or unpublished, to study and scrutiny.

The FDR years were painful indeed, but the Lord brought much good out of them. At Glacier View President Neal C. Wilson promised that the issues raised by Ford would be given thorough, on-going study. The Daniel and Revelation Committee, an international group of Adventists scholars, was a direct result. It met for nearly 10 years and prepared seven volumes of careful studies. While not all problems were solved, the church's teachings were placed on a stronger foundation than ever before. And the Davenport fiasco led to a review and tightening of the financial practices of the church.

FDR—I would not wish for those days of anger, disappointment, disillusionment, and pain to return. But through it all God was there, upholding His people, of that I am sure. Upholding me.

———————————

This is probably a good place to share a few reflections on the theological enterprise. I'll begin with a story.

On one of our numerous trips to Australia, a man contacted me by telephone, stating that he urgently needed to meet me. Since he lived close to Avondale College, we agreed to meet that Sabbath evening after I had concluded the meeting planned for me.

It was winter. By the time I was through greeting the people, the shadows were long and the air was turning cold. The deacons were locking the church, so he said, "Let's go and talk in my car." He had a small boy with him, but he told him, "Daddy has important business to discuss. You run around outside."

I wondered what could be so important. It turned out to be righteousness by faith. This man had views and questions that he wanted to put to me. So we talked—on and on we talked.

His boy came back, knocking on the window. "Daddy, I'm getting cold."

"Run around and keep warm."

We—mainly he—kept on talking. The boy returned. It was dark now. "Daddy, it's dark, and I'm cold."

"Daddy is busy. You look after yourself."

Eventually I couldn't stand any more. With great difficulty I restrained myself from letting go with both barrels, letting this man hear from me that his religion was a travesty. He was so full of his own ideas—on righteousness by faith, of all topics!—that he couldn't see that his little boy needed him.

As gracefully as I could, I abruptly terminated the conversation, and the man and his son drove away. But the scene lingers still in my head, illustrating vividly what is wrong with so much theological discussion.

Theology was my life for 20 years. I thought it was important. I still do.

But theology divorced from life is a failure. Theology can turn inward on itself. When theology becomes an end in itself, it becomes evil.

Adventists, by and large, manifest a keen interest in theological questions. That's good—but also deceptive. It's easy to fall into the trap of substituting correctness in theology for living a life like that of Jesus.

The study and teaching of theology exerts a bewitching power. In this above all areas of human study we need humility, but humility is the last quality theologians usually manifest. We are so sure our ideas are correct, must be correct, so that others can be shown to be wrong.

And we need each other when we do theology—that's the last observation I share. No one sees everything, no one understands perfectly. God has given a slice to each of us. He alone puts the slices all together. We need to listen to each other. We need to be open to gain insight from another's mind, from another's experience.

Three things abide, says Paul, only three. And the greatest isn't theology. It isn't even one of the three.

CHAPTER 10

Contending for the Faith

The time demands you, as pilots demand winds and a storm-tossed man a harbor,
in order to reach the presence of God.
—Letter of Ignatius to Polycarp, c. A.D. 110

By nature I am a reconciler, but at times my responsibilities at the
General Conference led me to take on the role of advocate and de-
fender. I love this church, imperfect as it is, built up over the years
by blood, sweat, and prayers, and if someone arises to tear it down,
I will set aside my natural inclination as peacemaker and go to bat
on behalf of the Adventist Church.

Given the controversies that characterized the 1980s, it isn't surprising that this period saw me for the first time adopt the role of de-
fender of the faith. In the later years of my tenure attacks on the
church leveled off, but they never ceased entirely. I expect that
Review editors before me found themselves compelled to contend
for the faith. Because of the high profile of the office, it is inevitable
that the editor at times will be challenged and thrust into the lime-
light. And the attacks originate from both outside the church and
from within.

—————◆◆◆—————

John Ankerberg is a Christian who hosts a television program devoted to matters of interest to evangelicals. Like other programs with similar format, *The John Ankerberg Show* thrives on
controversy and confrontation with the guests who appear.

In the early 1980s Ankerberg invited Desmond Ford to his program, and also Walter Rea. They leveled significant criticisms at the Seventh-day Adventist Church, concerning both its teachings and the conduct of its leaders. Ankerberg now wanted an official representative of the church to come before the cameras and respond to the charges that had been made by the earlier guests. He attempted to draw in a series of well-known Adventists, but all declined. With each refusal he added to the list he read aloud on his program, and it was getting embarrassing. Ankerberg was putting the Adventist Church in a bad light before those who watched his show on cable across America.

At length Ankerberg wrote to the General conference president himself, Neal C. Wilson. He rehearsed the list of those who had turned him down, then invited Wilson to take up the challenge. In the letter he added that, if Wilson could not appear, William Johnsson would be a satisfactory substitute. He sent a copy of the letter to me.

I read the letter with a rising sense of indignation. Throughout my ministry I have strongly believed that the teachings of this church can stand up to investigation, even the most withering by those who may not wish us well, that we have nothing to hide, and that we can bear our testimony in any forum. Although I was not a regular viewer of Ankerberg's show—we did not have cable TV at our home—what Ankerberg had shared in the letter made my blood boil. Something had to be done to meet his challenge. The leader of the world church should not step into the arena, which has high potential for manipulation, but someone else should take on Ankerberg. And he had suggested my name.

I went to Pastor Wilson and shared my conviction that this public shaming of the Adventist Church had to be met. I told him that he should never expose himself to the critics, but that I would offer myself if he wished. We talked the matter through and agreed that I should appear as the church's representative that Ankerberg had been publicly calling for. "It will be difficult, Bill," Wilson said. "You will face a no-win situation. They will try to trap you with the questions they put to you. But if you can just stay calm and sweet and make clear that as an Adventist you believe in righteousness by faith, that will be sufficient, whatever else they try to trick you into saying."

So I let Ankerberg know that I was willing to appear on his program. He explained the plan. Ankerberg would host the show, and there would be two guests—Walter Martin, who frequently appeared on the program, and I. A specialist in cults, Martin was relentless in exposing teachings at variance with the Scriptures, and he had knowledge of Adventists. Back in the 1950s he, along with *Eternity* editor Donald Barnhouse, had spent many hours discussing our doctrines with some Adventist leaders. As a result of these conversations, Martin had removed Adventists from his list of cults. On the Adventist side, the book *Questions on Doctrine* (itself a lightning rod for some Adventists) had been produced and circulated widely. But by the 1980s the book was out of print. Martin wanted to know if we intended to reprint it, or, as he began to allege, we had backed off from the positions taken in the book.

So here was another element in the critical mix of the times: not just Ford and Rea, but Walter Martin. The latter was writing church leaders to see if we had gone cold on *Questions on Doctrine*—in which case he was considering reclassifying Adventism among the cults. Likewise in public meetings Martin was becoming more critical of the Adventist Church, especially singling out Ellen White and her writings for censure.

Having been involved with Ford and Rea firsthand, I had a sense of the questions I might expect in the areas they had raised. And tapes of Martin's meetings were available for me to listen to in anticipation of the Ankerberg show. Martin frequently threw out this question to Adventists: "Do you believe that Ellen White is an infallible interpreter of Scripture—yes or no?" I figured I would hear that one before we got very far on the Ankerberg set.

The producer of the program wrote me about plans and details. They would pay my airfare to Chattanooga, Tennessee, where the program would be taped, and put me up in a motel. I should arrive on a Sunday night, early so as to be fresh for the show, which would take place the following evening. Monday I would join Ankerberg and Martin for lunch. We would get acquainted and go over plans for the program. A live audience would be present.

Everything seemed in order. I consented to the arrangements. So a Sunday night in December 1984 saw me flying into Chattanooga, where the producer was on hand to meet me. He took me to the motel and I settled in for the night, a bit apprehensive as to what the new day might bring. This would be my first-ever appearance on television. But, as the events unfolded the next day, that would be the least of my worries.

Shortly before lunch the producer called me. The planned meeting was off. We would instead meet at supper. A little alarm bell sounded in my head. It rang louder when later in the day I received another telephone call—the supper meeting had also been canceled for some reason. What was going on here? I went to the studio with uneasy feelings, hoping for the best but concerned that I was about to enter an unexpected and hostile arena.

I met Ankerberg and Martin just before we went on camera. All the assurances about getting acquainted, etc., went down the toilet. There was just time for makeup and testing sound levels, and we were live.

Ankerberg and Martin presented a study in contrasts. The former's hair fascinated me because of its extremely blond color. *Could it be real?* I wondered. Martin, a much older person, was dark-haired and burly. A large metal cross hung from his neck. As he became animated on the show, the cross swung back and forth, bumping against the microphone. The producer asked him to take off the cross.

The program would be taped in 15-minute segments, with short breaks in between, and a longer period halfway through the show. Then the cameras started to roll.

After introducing the program and guests, Ankerberg handed off to Walter Martin. He began with a long list of charges and criticisms, throwing together statements from detractors of the church and quotations culled from Adventist writings over many years. He went on and on. It was a formidable barrage. At last he stopped, and Ankerberg invited me to respond. I began to tackle some of the issues, but suddenly the producer called, "Cut! Time to break."

As they were changing the tapes, I went to the producer. "What is going on?" I wanted to know. "Martin gets 10 minutes to make his charges, and I get only two minutes to reply?"

By now I knew it was going to be a long night. And it was. The program, which began so unpromisingly, only got worse for me.

Very soon I became deeply disappointed in the role played by Ankerberg. I expected him to take a basically neutral stance. Instead he joined with Martin in aggressive questioning. Martin, I knew, would raise questions and issues, but to my consternation the host became the chief interrogator. During breaks Ankerberg and Martin huddled, comparing questions they had prepared on flash cards, planning the line of attack they would take during the next segment.

Inside I was beginning to boil. The format, from my perspective, seemed grossly unfair. The line of questioning did not attempt to give a balanced picture of what Adventists stood for. It was all on the side of faults, criticisms, and alleged errors. And this was purportedly a Christian television show? Yes, the name of Jesus was mentioned, along with references to the Bible and various Christian doctrines, but the attitude, the spirit of the show, was overwhelmingly negative, designed to put the Seventh-day Adventist Church in a bad light.

Martin frequently interrupted me. During one of the breaks I complained about it to the producer. "Look," I said, "I let Martin have his say, but when I get the microphone he butts in and takes over." His reply: "Well, you'll just have to do the same to him." Well and good if you're that sort of person, but to me it was a breach of good manners to which I refused to consent, on live television or elsewhere.

During another break Martin and Ankerberg laughingly related the experience of a previous guest. Under the heat of the questioning about the church she represented, she took off her microphone and stormed from the set. Of course, that made for good audience appeal. "We're being easy on you tonight," said Martin, "because you're a brother," but I had the strong impression that he and Ankerberg would not have been unhappy had I followed the example of the woman guest before me.

The questions covered the gamut: prophecy, the heavenly sanctuary, the pre-Advent judgment, and especially Ellen White. Martin and Ankerberg had a file of quotations from Adventist publications, including the *Adventist Review*. Some of the statements they read had appeared in print many years ago; others were more recent. In each case the quotations set forth, or appeared to set forth, a position at variance with biblical, orthodox theology. These statements, frankly, were embarrassing to me.

In responding to these challenges—and they were many and varied—I tried to point out that Adventists have many publishing houses and print many books and magazines. We do not have any censorship board that vets the content of our publications, so occasionally one can find ideas that reflect the views of a particular editor rather than the official position of the Seventh-day Adventist Church. Only the Statement of Fundamental Beliefs (at that time 27 in number; now 28) states correctly what the world Adventist Church believes.

I repeated this line of defense over and over: "Yes, you may find that statement in a book or magazine published at some time in our history. But it is *not* our official position. The 27 fundamental beliefs state that . . . ."

I was never more grateful for the fundamental beliefs than that night.

As I expected, Martin wanted to know whether the church had repudiated *Questions on Doctrine*. When I replied that we had not, he spent some time trying to draw me out as to why the book had not been reprinted.

And his stock charge that we believe that Ellen White was an infallible interpreter of Scripture also came up. After a long buildup, Martin put the question to me directly. I gave a short, crisp reply: "We do not believe that Ellen White was an infallible interpreter of Scripture."

"What!" he rejoined. "But so and so said . . . and . . . and . . . ."

"That may be so," I countered, "but that is not the church's official position." Eventually Martin and Ankerberg moved on to other lines of questioning.

With both these key issues—*Questions on Doctrine* and the role of Ellen White—I could have embellished my reply. I could have told Martin, "I asked our world leader, Neal C. Wilson, that very same question—whether the church has repudiated *Questions on Doctrine*—and he stated that we have not. I asked Robert Olson, secretary of the Ellen G. White, whether he believes that Ellen White was an infallible interpreter of Scripture, and he does not." But I chose not to piggyback on anyone else's convictions. I took my stand as an individual Adventist, ready to answer from the heart.

The evening went on and on. Somehow I got through it, but only by the Lord's grace. Just for a few minutes I found a respite—Martin moved into the book of Hebrews. Soon, however, he realized that I was well versed in that area, so he dropped Hebrews and went to a different subject.

Throughout the show Ankerberg kept announcing that the audience would be given opportunity to ask their questions. As the time passed, I wondered if this part of the program would ever take place. Right at the close, however, it did.

Several people lined up to speak, and my heart sang when the first person announced that he was a Seventh-day Adventist minister. At last—a friendly question would come my way! But I was in for another rude shock. Instead of the softball I expected, I heard another attack on the sanctuary doctrine and Ellen White.

It was, perhaps, the most trying moment in a long, trying evening. I was nonplussed. I could hardly believe my ears, and struggled to frame a coherent response.

Later, long after the evening was over and the program aired, I discovered more about the questioner. He had misrepresented himself. He had once been an Adventist pastor, but was no longer serving in ministry. How and why he came to the taping that night I do not know and did not try to find out. Nor did I pursue the possibility that he might have been "planted" in the audience to embarrass me. Whether or not that was the case, his questions certainly discombobulated me.

At last, mercifully, it was all over. I returned to the motel, but not to sleep. All through the night my mind replayed the dynamic—the interrogation and my responses. In the heat of the battle, with interlocutors on both right and left, had I said something that could be used to embarrass the church I loved? I could not think of any serious slip, but the possibility that one had occurred plagued my rest.

We taped for several hours that Monday evening. The material was edited into several 30-minute programs. In the process there was considerable rearrangement. For instance, clips of the questioners lined up at the microphones were inserted to give the impression that these people were there from the beginning, whereas they got their chance only right at the close. Although the material was chopped up and reconfigured, the editing was fair, and my ideas weren't distorted. I noticed, however, that those parts of the program in which I scored points on Martin, such as his venture into the book of Hebrews, were deleted from the segments that went out to viewers.

Several months after the taping the programs began to air. They have aired—and aired! I still receive mail from people who write that they saw me on *The John Ankerberg Show,* thinking that it happened recently. I tell them the show was taped in 1984 and went on the air the following year. The segments even found their way to the Internet. "Do you know you're on YouTube?" I've been asked.

Why these segments continue to have life puzzles me. But for one thing I am especially grateful to the Lord. He protected me from any unguarded statement that might have embarrassed the Adventist Church for many years beyond. As mad as I felt inside, He kept me calm and composed, right to the trying end.

Not everyone was pleased with what they saw on TV. Adventists who thought *Questions on Doctrine* was a bad book disliked my public statement that the church had not repudiated it. Others who held a particular view of Ellen White's inspiration (one that she herself did not advocate) thought I had failed her miserably. So I received plenty of letters letting me know I had blown it.

But there were some on the other side. One of the most affirming came from Edward Fudge, an evangelical attorney in Houston, Texas. He sent me a long letter in which he gave his assessment of the show. After pointing out that he was not an Adventist, he wanted me to know that I had comported myself in a truly Christian manner. "In fact," he wrote, "you were the only Christian on the program."

Would I do it again? Yes. As difficult as the experience was, I would do it again, because I believe that there is a time to go public with what Adventists believe, even if the deck is stacked against us, even if it looks like a setup.

But I would make sure one aspect was different. I would have in the audience someone—at least one person—to whom I could look and know that they were a friend and praying for me. Walter Martin had his cheering section in the audience, and he played up to it. I felt dreadfully on my own.

But I was not on my own. The Lord was there, by my side, right through.

———◦◆◦———

Especially during the 1980s and 1990s many new Adventist organizations arose. Most were committed to mission and followed a cooperative relationship with the official church. With many lay-initiated ministries, Adventist-laymen's Services and Industries grew rapidly into a powerful body with branches outside North America. Its annual convention, dynamic and focused on sharing experiences of witnessing, became an event that church administrators did not want to miss.

Some groups, comparatively few in number, adopted a critical stance, however. Faulting both leaders and official doctrinal positions, they produced publications to promote their views. These groups encompassed both right-wing ("conservative") and left-wing ("liberal") views.

With competing positions vying for the minds and allegiance of members and ministers, I tried hard to keep the *Review* in the solid center. It wasn't easy. A lot of my time went into answering letters, endeavoring to help the people to keep from being blown away by the winds of doctrine that swirled around them. The effort was necessary, but often I felt sad that so much of my time and energy had to go toward a remedial work instead of positive initiatives.

Very early in my experience I had come up against critics of the church and with surprise had discerned how they often went about their business. One of my classmates during my Avondale days was Robert Brinsmead. Possessed of a keen mind, he quoted verbatim not only Scripture but passages from Ellen White, attracting a number of students to Bible studies he held in his room. One day the senior Bible teacher, Pastor Nelson Burns, came to class in an agitated frame of mind. He appealed to us not to stir up the congregations with controversial material when we went on preaching assignments. Later we learned that it was Brinsmead who, presenting topics such as Armageddon, had upset the people.

As we came to the senior year of ministerial training, the college authorities presented Brinsmead with an ultimatum: he would not be permitted to register unless he agreed to abstain from controversial areas. Brinsmead declined to do so. He moved out of the dorm and rented a house near the entrance to the college. From this base he continued to meet students and others.

At the end of the year, when I went home to Adelaide, my father showed me some advertising material. "I see there's going to be a combined meeting," he said. He had received a brochure announcing a visit by certain "leaders" and wondered who they were—he'd never heard of them. A quick look, and the picture was immediately clear to me. These weren't representatives of the church at all, but part of the offshoot movement with Brinsmead at the center. I assured my dad that the advertised meeting was quite different from what he had thought. The approach used by the dissidents bothered me, however. If they could dupe my godly father, who knows how many others might be taken in?

Now, a quarter century later, I was witnessing a rerun. Without exception the critical groups presented themselves as bona fide Seventh-day Adventists. Their papers used our jargon. They dropped names of church leaders. They played up any visit to General Conference headquarters. And much of what they printed touched a chord, especially as they called for revival and reformation. But here was the rub—a negative, critical tone pervaded the writing. You could not read much of the material without concluding that the church was on the wrong track and that many, if not most, of its ministers were poor shepherds.

Some of these groups expanded their activities to include separate camp meetings and rallies. They roundly criticized the Statement of Fundamental Beliefs, wanting one of their main emphases—that Jesus was born with a sinful nature—to be included. And they went further. They began accepting members' tithes. With this they had become a parachurch organization. They were functioning as a separate church but still claiming to be Seventh-day Adventists.

For many of our people, it was a confusing time. I prayed long and hard for wisdom and grace to meet the needs of the day. The church *did* have many faults—this was correct. But God still loved the church, flawed though it was (and is!). The way of Jesus is to build up in love, not to tear down. And I believe that in a free church press, if an individual or a group wants to start their own publication, they have a right to do so. Only be transparently honest, making clear what the new paper is about, and how it is funded.

One day I decided to blow the whistle on some of these groups and publications that to my mind were duping church members, just as my dear dad had been duped long before. I composed an editorial in question-and-answer form, naming organizations and giving the facts. It was time to let the people know the truth on individuals and "ministries" that preyed on the church like parasites, that could not exist were it not for the very church they criticized.

The editorial went into production. It was set in type, scheduled for printing. Then, as a precaution, I ran a copy by my friend, attorney Bob Nixon, chief counsel for the General Conference. He did not find any legal problem with the material, but he posed a question: "If you print this, you will spend the rest of your time as editor dealing with these people, who will focus their attacks on you. Are you sure that is what you want to do?"

I thought about it. He was right.

I tore up the editorial. The *Adventist Review*, instead of pointing out the faults of others, would concentrate on giving a positive message. I would let the Lord deal with the critics.

I glanced over my list of appointments for the day, and looked again. Scheduled to meet with me was a person whom I had never encountered but knew all too well by name.

This man, who had served in the Adventist ministry for a short time, had become one of the church's most strident critics. With donations flowing into his coffers from church members, he had rapidly built up a mini-empire based on the media. A charismatic TV speaker, he had purchased two TV trucks from which he could record or transmit programs. He bought out a radio network. He had his own church and a large staff. He also had established a flourishing school.

For a short time he backed off from attacking the Seventh-day Adventist Church. The offerings took a nosedive, and shortly thereafter he resumed the criticism and the money flowed again.

I had felt the sting of his man's attacks. In an issue of the *Review* we had reported on a gathering of Hispanic Adventists and ran a photograph of the meeting on the cover. This cover came under pointed attack by the critical televangelist. He printed a scathing article that claimed the photograph pictured a Roman Catholic priest. Of course, it did not—the person singled out was dressed out in traditional Hispanic garb. The critic, however, followed up with a long video that he sent out to his supporters. See how brazen this Johnsson has become, the video said—so brazen that Johnsson even puts a picture of a Catholic priest on the cover!

Several people wrote or telephoned me about the attacks on me and the church paper, and in a low-key fashion I tried to set the record straight through the pages of the *Review*. And now this man was coming to my office?

The meeting took a turn I could not have dreamed of. When the critic showed up, he brought his wife along, and immediately began to apologize and beg for forgiveness. We had a long, tearful, amazing session together. He confessed his wrongs toward me and other church leaders whom he had attacked, and wanted to know if he might buy an ad in the *Review* to publicly confess and apologize. I told him that I did not think that was a good idea. Instead, he should contact personally those whom he had wronged.

Overjoyed at what I was hearing, I was eager to learn what had brought about his sharp change of heart. He recounted how he had planned a certain broadcast denouncing the Seventh-day Adventist church as Babylon. But just before going before the cameras, he happened to pick up a book of selections from Ellen White's writings. How the book found its way to the room he could not tell, but he thumbed through it. The pages opened to a message warning in strong terms against calling the church Babylon. Shocked and rebuked, he canceled the broadcast.

In time, this event led to a reversal in his preaching—and his fortunes. He stopped attacking the church, and the offerings fell away. At length he lost the TV trucks, the church, the radio network, the school, his staff—everything. And now he was attempting to do what he could to set matters right.

I had quickly forgiven him; now I tried to minister to him. He was burdened with the thought that he had betrayed his calling to the ministry, that the church would never give him another chance. A text came to mind and I read it to him: "So I will restore to you the years that the swarming locust has eaten" (Joel 2:25, NKJV). "God is able to make up for the lost years," I told him. "God can give you a new start."

The words of Scripture came to him like a life buoy tossed to someone drowning. He reached out to them, hoping against hope that they might be fulfilled in his life. I can never forget the power and passion of that moment as a ray of light pierced his being.

I told him that the way back would not be easy. Some people would find it difficult to forgive and accept him. I urged him to keep a low profile and show the genuineness of his change of heart by accepting any responsibility, no matter how lowly.

And he did. This man, who not long before had ruled a mini-empire, learned to eat humble pie. He scrabbled, as it were, to provide for his family. The months passed.

Then one day I received a call from a conference president. They needed someone to shepherd two small churches, and he was considering hiring this man. What did I think? Should he give him a chance?

I told him I hoped he would. He did. And now, many years later, this same brother still serves in ministry, faithfully building up the church that he had once attacked.

I received many letters in the *Review* office, and once e-mail came along, the number of messages multiplied. During the years I served as editor, three wonderful assistants worked with me—Corinne Russ, Chitra Barnabas, and Rachel Child—and each received the same instruction: show me all the letters. Don't keep back anything, no matter how vitriolic.

In reality, my mail ran about 90 percent positive. Even correspondents who had a beef with something that appeared in the church paper would often add ". . . but you're doing a good job." Some letters, however, arrived smoking hot, requiring asbestos gloves to handle them. And often, it seemed, they came on Monday morning!

Throughout my tenure I gave the mail priority. I spent a lot of time reading and replying to letters, even in later years when the work of the office had expanded greatly and time was exceedingly precious. During the early period I often gave lengthy replies, answering the correspondent point by point. After a while I came to realize that this approach simply invited the other to come back at me with a new series of arguments. At length I learned to answer in the manner of H. L. Mencken: "Dear Sir, you may be right." I found that a gracious answer that put the best construction on the blast I had received frequently produced surprising results. Sometimes I would hear back with the request to destroy or return the negative letter I had been sent.

Telephone calls were more difficult to handle in a Christlike manner. The more the person on the other end lashed out at me and the church, the more I felt like replying in kind. Some critical calls went on and on . . . and on. I inwardly struggled to find a way to bring the blast to an end. During one conversation I broke in with "Listen, my friend, this telephone call is going nowhere. Let's just stop and pray together." At least that approach brought a pause at the other end.

I didn't handle some of these conversations well. Too defensive. Too judgmental. Too slow to listen, too quick to snap back. Too much relying on my own wisdom. Too little waiting on the Lord.

But there were good outcomes. People who called back later to thank me or to apologize, or to say how patiently I had heard them out. The Lord can do wonders through the feeble, flawed vessels He has to use!

CHAPTER 11

Women In Ministry

RESOLVED, That females possessing the necessary qualifications to fill the position, may, with perfect propriety, be set apart by ordination to the work of the Christian ministry.
—Action of the General Conference Session, December 5, 1881

After so many years the words jump out from the small type of the *Review and Herald*. The questions tumble out: What was the background to the resolution? Did Ellen White support or oppose it? What happened to the action subsequently?

The issues for the *Review* prior to this startling action contain no hint of a discussion, let alone debate, concerning the appropriateness of women in ministry. We do find, however, occasional articles that take up passages that could be used to oppose women ministers, such as 1 Corinthians 14:34, in which Paul counsels that women should keep silent in church. The writers in the *Review and Herald* considered the biblical context and concluded that such passages cannot legitimately be used to keep women from speaking in church.

There was, of course, one Adventist woman who spoke in church, who spoke a great deal, and from the pulpit—Ellen G. White. But she was not alone. Examination of archival material has established that women played a prominent role in the early Adventist Church. Several women occupied the post of General Conference treasurer. Others served as pastors and evangelists and carried ministerial licenses. It was probably inevitable that the question of their ordination to the ministry would eventually come to the fore.

When the resolution supporting women's ordination came to the 1881 General Conference session, Ellen White, although present, did not voice an opinion. The item in the *Review and Herald*, brief as it is, simply states after the action: "This was discussed by J. O. Corliss, A. C. Bourdeau, E. R. Jones, D. A. Lamson, W. H. Littlejohn, A. S. Hutchins, D. M. Cainwright, and J. N. Loughborough, and referred to the General Conference committee."

Was the action passed? The terse report leaves the issue open. The *Signs of the Times* also reported on the resolution, stating that it was passed. However, the absence of a specific statement to this effect in the *Review and Herald* leads many church historians to conclude that it did not receive a formal vote.

The action was referred to the General Conference Committee for follow up. But here the matter disappears from view. No evidence has ever been located that the General Conference Committee discussed the resolution or took action on it. So this fascinating chapter from the early days of the church fades into history.

A point of interest as we leave it: the General Conference Committee at that time consisted of just three people. All were males.

———•◆•———

Exactly a century later the issue of women in ministry again came to the fore. Especially in North America, it generated strong feelings and at times fierce debate. Three General conference sessions addressed the matter—those in 1985, 1990, and 1995. Letters, pro and con ordination of women, poured into the *Review*. All this took place on my watch. It became the hottest topic the *Review* handled.

As had been the case before the 1881 discussion, women had become involved in ministerial leadership. During the 1970s the church in North America took a series of steps that seemed destined to put women on a course that would in time lead to ordination to the gospel ministry. First, the doors opened for women to be ordained as elders of the local church. They then were given opportunity to participate in ministry as assistant pastors, and then to receive ministerial scholarships at the seminary.

All these developments took place in the North American Division, with Neal C. Wilson as president, and without reference to a General Conference session. Over the years Wilson has championed the cause of minorities and underdogs—notably on behalf of Black Adventists, and on the side of women. Since Neal Wilson weighs decisions carefully and tries to anticipate their immediate and long-term impact, I can only conclude that he foresaw that the course he had encouraged over several years inevitably would lead to the question of women's ordination to the gospel ministry, as it had a century earlier.

In the 1980s, however, Wilson's thinking seems to have undergone a shift. Now leader of the world church, he decided that the question of women's ordination was one that the world church— that is, a General Conference session—must adjudicate. The reasoning advanced was that since we are a global church, ministers can be called to serve anywhere, and therefore ordination must have universal validity. Whether Wilson entertained this view all along or whether someone convinced him of it after he became General Conference president, I do not know. The course he followed during the 1970s suggests to me that it was the latter.

The decision to refer the issue to the general body had profound repercussions. The question could no longer be settled along merely theological lines, if it ever could. Cultural norms now became a highly charged element of the discussion.

During the years 1984 to 2005, proponents and opponents waged a war of words, turning out articles, pamphlets, and even books. A new magazine, *Adventists Affirm*, arose to champion the con side. Emotions ran high, especially among women. The debates at the 1990 and 1995 General Conference sessions in particular left many women feeling wounded, angry, insulted, disappointed, and exposed as objects of discussion by men. On the other hand, the strongest opposition I observed came from women, especially older women. In a dynamic that I did not understand, they felt threatened by the prospect of women being ordained as clergy.

In the *Adventist Review* office, convictions varied among the staff. The editors weren't of one mind, and although I strongly supported the pro side, I did not try to impose my views on the others. I tried to be evenhanded in dealing with the controversial topic, letting editors express themselves but ensuring that the *Review* did not become a partisan voice. One magazine issue addressed the issue head-on: the cover depicted a woman in the pulpit, with the inside featuring parallel articles by proponents and opponents of women's ordination. The issue brought a flood of mail.

Some of my former colleagues in academia thought that the *Review* should give a lead to the church. In their eyes here was a righteous cause that the church paper should champion, just as it had in the early years of the Adventist Church when it opposed slavery and called for civil disobedience to the fugitive slave law. On the other hand, some Adventists thought the *Review* shouldn't sit on the fence but adopt a stance against a position that Scripture forbade.

That was the dilemma. Good, sincere Adventists were on both sides—and Scripture did not give a clear-cut answer. The Bible neither commends nor condemns ordination of women to the gospel ministry. At best the Bible supplies hints of principles that might be applied, and scattered texts of a mixed nature.

What to do with the essential silence of Scripture on the topic—this was the nub of the debate. Because the Bible does not forbid the ordination of women but rather tells us that in Christ there is no longer Jew nor Greek, bond nor free, male nor female, does not the church, led by the Spirit, have the freedom to go ahead? But dare we, a people who look to the Bible for our beliefs and practices, go ahead without a clear "Thus saith the Lord" that women may be ordained?

Lacking a definitive biblical answer, Adventists in the 1980s and 1990s—and today, though much less so—go back and forth with argument and counterargument. In the *Review* office the letters pretty soon ran dry of new material. They simply rehashed previous positions.

At times the level of reasoning, in letters and in public discussions, lacked depth and biblical study. Many times I saw and heard what those opposed to women's ordination argued was a strong text for their case—1 Timothy 3:2, in which Paul counsels that an elder "must be the husband of one wife." Since a woman cannot meet this requirement, she is by definition excluded from the office of elder— so the reasoning went.

But the text teaches no such thing. The expression "*one* wife" shows us Paul's intent. He counsels that an elder must not have more than one wife. That is the only issue. To use this passage against the ordination of women would disqualify Paul himself, since, as he makes clear, he was single! (1 Cor. 7:7, 8; 9:5, 6).

———————◆◆◆———————

In preparation for the 1985 session, Wilson appointed a commission to study the issue. A large group, it included all the world division presidents plus a variety of other people selected to represent the range of opinions. I was part of this commission, as well as of the second one that was appointed following the 1985 session.

As *Review* editor I felt the need to be fair and impartial. As commission member I felt it my obligation to freely express my convictions on the subject. This led me to speak forthrightly about the moral aspect of the issue of women's ordination. At the time the commission was engaged in a discussion of whether the issue was theological or moral. I pointed out that such an either-or approach was faulty. While the issue involved theology, it also involved justice. Reminding commission members that too often theology had been used to deny ethical action—as with the history of slavery in the United States or the defense of apartheid in South Africa—I argued that theology cannot trump morality.

To me, the question of women's ordination was a moral issue. I still hold that opinion. When, as I saw, two people graduate from the Master of Divinity course at the seminary, enter into pastoral ministry, serve successfully in different churches in the same conference, but after several years one was ordained and the other was not simply because of gender, is not the situation patently unjust? No amount of theological reasoning can diminish such unfair treatment.

My speech to the commission caused a stir. I did not think any more about it until the following day, when the chair, Elder Wilson, began the session by referring to it. He told the group that the division presidents had discussed it that morning before the meeting, and some felt that I had singled them out. Then he invited me to respond. I said that the views I had stated were meant to express my own convictions; that I realized that others saw the matter differently, and I respected their convictions; and that I had no intention whatsoever to single out any individual who differed from me in this matter.

During the deliberations of the first commission, Wilson did not tip his hand. Those on each side probably thought he inclined to their view. He seemed content to let all points of view and arguments be given a hearing. And so the commission came to a close without reaching a conclusion.

Thus, the 1985 General Conference session witnessed no debate on the matter. Delegates merely received a report of the commission and were informed that discussions would continue, with a recommendation to come to the 1990 session. During the period between the sessions each division was to canvass its various fields as to their likely reaction to ordained women clergy.

Wilson set up a second commission to meet and prepare a recommendation. Many of the members carried over from the first commission. We met in March 1988 and then, with great anticipation on the part of some of us, we gathered at the Cohutta Springs, Georgia, retreat center for the decisive meeting in July 1989.

One by one, the division presidents reported on studies in their fields. The results varied dramatically—from almost 100 percent acceptance of women ministers to almost 100 percent rejection. Some divisions, such as the Trans-European Division, had found huge differences within their own territory.

Then the discussion commenced. I expected a spirited give-and-take, a probing of the arguments on either side to assess their strengths and weaknesses. Instead, I was greatly disappointed. The chair (Wilson) simply permitted any and all to make their speech. The result was a long string of remarks, given in random order without rebuttal. When at last one's turn came up on the chair's list, points and arguments presented long before and crying out for a response had been forgotten by the brain-weary commission members.

It was one of the most frustrating exercises in which I have ever engaged. I was disappointed in Wilson, and puzzled why he had chosen to conduct the meeting in this disorganized fashion.

As the hours and days wore on, I began to discern where Wilson was headed. Apparently—no doubt in consultation with the division presidents and his fellow officers—he had decided that no consensus was possible. So the commission's recommendation to the General Conference session would be *to make no recommendation*. The status quo would continue. The session would be asked not to approve the ordination of women ministers, but neither would it be asked to roll back the steps taken years before that permitted women to serve in pastoral ministry.

The following year the General Conference session convened in Indianapolis, Indiana. This was *the* issue on the agenda, and long lines formed at the microphones. Given the strong emotions on both sides of the issue, a fair, firm moderator was called for, and the Lord provided one in a General Conference vice president, Calvin B. Rock. With goodwill and humor he guided the lengthy debate with an unerring hand.

Eventually the council adopted the position coming from the commission. Because of the lack of consensus in the world church in favor of ordination of women in ministry, the church would not sanction this final step in the process that began nearly 20 years before. But—a logical and theological contradiction—the session also voted that where divisions so authorize, women may be ordained as local elders and serve as ministers, performing all the functions integral to ministry. That is, women may preside at the Lord's Supper, baptize, and officiate at weddings. With the second action, what had already been permitted for North America was extended to the world church.

These two actions, to some extent running counter to each other, led to much confusion. For many people, especially those who did not attend the 1990 session or read carefully its actions, the whole debate collapsed into one issue—ordination. The delegates, by clear vote, had rejected it; therefore, women ministers also had been rejected. Some Adventists extended this wrong understanding of the session's actions to reject women as local church elders also. Thus, in the years following the session, women ministers found themselves tagged with rebellion because they were in defiance of the 1990 General Conference session action. Likewise at the *Review*. Whenever we printed news that involved women in ministry, angry letters flowed in charging us with supporting the insubordination in the North American Division. Kindly but firmly I pointed out that it was we, not they, whose position conformed to the vote of the session. Once a leader of an overseas field waited for me, smoke coming from his nostrils, because of a picture we had run of a woman baptizing. When I took out the 1990 *Bulletin* and read him the actual actions, he spluttered in disbelief.

Indianapolis did not bring down the curtain on the issue of women in ministry. With more women clergy practicing in North America and feelings running high, the North American Division leadership requested that the next General Conference session grant each division the authority to settle the ordination question in terms of what best met the needs of its territory. Thus, the focus shifted from ordination to the latitude to be granted any division. However, as the session drew near and then at the session itself, the immediate issue collapsed into the controverted question of ordination.

The 1995 General Conference session convened in Utrecht in the Netherlands. Once again Rock chaired the debate on the hot topic. Once again he exhibited fairness, firmness, impartiality, and grace. Two speakers, both professors at the Seventh-day Adventist Theological Seminary at Andrews University, were selected beforehand to present the arguments pro and con. Afterward the floor would be opened for debate.

The presentations provided a classic demonstration in mass persuasion. On one hand, the person chosen to give the pro side set out a scholarly, reasoned, qualified case. On the other side, the presenter followed a literal—some said literalistic—proof text approach with texts on overheads that matched the minds of many delegates.

When the session was opened to speeches, long lines formed at the microphones. It was not the church's finest hour. Some speeches demeaned women, and a competitive spirit ran through the assembly. Many women left the meeting feeling put down and badly bruised.

Just prior to the vote on the motion, the General Conference president Robert S. Folkenberg made remarks, as he had promised to do. Up to this point the reaction of delegates to the two presentations and the speeches showed that the con viewpoint had very strong support. Perhaps, however, the world church leader would share counsel that might change the outcome. Folkenberg spoke for several minutes, but at the close of his remarks it was impossible to tell which side he favored. Perhaps, given the dynamic of the occasion, that was the wisest course for him to pursue.

The request from the North American Division lost overwhelmingly. In the aftermath and for years following some Adventists said that the 1995 session voted to deny women a place in ministry, but that was never the issue in Utrecht.

The whole proceeding left a bad taste in the mouths of the North American delegation. They viewed, with some justification, the debate and the vote as being as much an anti-American gesture as a discussion of the merits of the case. In the evening following the debate, the North American Division section was noticeably empty in the assembly hall, as many American delegates gathered in large and small groups to lick their wounds. Women delegates in particular felt angry and insulted by speeches of some of the overseas delegates.

Into this situation, ripe for long-term damage to the unity of the world church, stepped North American Division president Al McClure. Years before he had opposed women's ordination, but had changed his view after studying the arguments, and it was he who brought the North American Division request to the session. Now, rising to the occasion, he acted the part of a church statesman. That Wednesday evening even some of his union presidents, incensed at what had transpired, were threatening to pull their students from the seminary, but McClure called together the entire North American Division delegation and restored calm and clear reasoning.

Within a couple of months of the Utrecht vote the Sligo church in Takoma Park, Maryland, ordained three women to the gospel ministry. Other ordinations followed at La Sierra, Loma Linda, and elsewhere. None of these ordination services had official approval of the church—not by conference or union conference, let alone the division.

We reported these developments in the *Review*. Letters continued to pour in, some of them strongly worded. We printed a cross-section. After several months, however, I concluded that continuing the debate in the church paper did not serve the church well. No new arguments were forthcoming—it was a rehash of old stuff. And the North American field, already polarized, was being torn apart by accusation and counteraccusation. It was time to go on. I announced to readers that, while the *Review* would continue to carry news items related to ordination of women, we would cut off all letters and articles on the topic.

Since 1995 much of the heat over this issue has dissipated in the

North American Division. I think, however, that the church has paid a heavy price. Young people and young adults—how many, only the Lord knows—simply walked away from a church that they perceived to be lacking in essential justice. Painfully, I saw this firsthand. Once when I told my own children about the discussions of the commissions, they exclaimed, "Dad, what is there to talk about?"

But women continue in ministry, and their numbers increase more and more. Several divisions now have their own women ministers, while in China (so I have been told) women play a major—perhaps leading—role, not only in ministry but in administration. At least one of these women leaders is officially ordained to the gospel ministry. And Africa, which strongly opposed ordination of women in 1990 and 1995, shows evidence of a change in thinking.

In North America women serve as ministers with all the prerogatives of male ministers—the only exception being authority to organize churches. They receive identical compensation to their male counterparts. Most have been set apart by a commissioning service. Is the issue therefore moot?

No. Although many women prepare for ministry by taking the Master of Divinity course at the seminary, they have a more difficult time in being hired. Many congregations simply don't want a woman—any woman—to be their spiritual shepherd, which creates difficulties for conference administrators. And absent ordination, many members do not view women ministers in the same light as ordained male clergy.

———◆———

As I reflect on this fascinating chapter in Adventist history, I cannot help wondering what the outcome might have been if the debate had proceeded along different lines. I do not fault our leaders who sought to guide the church through this controversial issue, but in looking back, a glaring fault stands out. We debated the ordination of women without first coming to clarity on the meaning and purpose of ordination itself. A wide range of views existed, and still exist, among us. We put the cart before the horse.

The Bible says comparatively little on the topic. We read about the laying on of hands for deacons, elders, and missionaries. But the Bible says nothing regarding an ordination service for ministers per se. In fact, there is no specific, separate word signifying ordination to the ministry.

We Adventists see ourselves as heirs of the Reformation, and we might have learned much from the Reformers' views on ordination. They had a "low" view, because they had revolted against the priest-ridden system of the large church and wanted at all costs to keep Protestant ministers from being regarded as having sacerdotal authority. They taught the priesthood of *all* believers. They viewed ordination of the clergy as something that the state called for in order to recognize who was authorized to serve as a minister.

In North America no doubt a range of views on ordination prevail among Adventists. Some regard the minister with veneration similar to that accorded a priest, but most probably do not. Most would find it difficult to express just what ordination signifies.

Around the globe a similar spectrum of views can be found. Adventists who live in areas in which the Roman Catholic Church has major influence understandably tend toward a "high" view of ordination and the ministry. We as a church have never addressed this question in a careful, intentional manner. Maybe it is time that we did.

Women will continue in ministry, of this I am quite sure. Their numbers will increase, as they should, because the task is too great for us to neglect any resource that the Lord has provided. Women bring to ministry unique qualities of caring and nurturing.

The ordination issue is unfinished business for the Seventh-day Adventist Church. It was unfinished in 1881, and it remains unfinished. But don't look for it to come up for discussion at a General Conference session in the foreseeable future.

CHAPTER 12

The Swelling of Jordan

If thou hast run with the footmen, and they have wearied thee,
then how canst thou contend with horses?
and if in the land of peace, wherein thou trustedst,
they wearied thee, then how wilt thou do in the swelling of Jordan?
—Jeremiah 12:5, KJV

C*risis* is a word I rarely use. But in the first months of 1999 the
Seventh-day Adventist Church faced a situation with issues of such
gravity and the outcome so uncertain that indeed a crisis was upon
us. And, unlike the difficult Kellogg period early in the twentieth
century, we no longer had the Lord's messenger to provide counsel.

Almost no one saw what loomed on the horizon. The waters of
Jordan were rising, slowly and inexorably, and we were blissfully
unaware. Life went on at the *Adventist Review* office and the General
Conference as it had before, as it seemed certain to continue. But
soon Jordan would reach flood tide and burst its banks.

Looking back, there were a couple of signs that something was
wrong. Robert Nixon, chief legal counsel for the General Conference,
was and is a close personal friend. The Johnsson and Nixon families
usually vacationed together at the beach every summer, and we got
together again in 1998. Bob Nixon is a pleasant man with a delightful
sense of humor. But that year at the beach he seemed a different person. He spent most of the time alone on the deck of the condo next
to ours, hardly saying a word. It was so unlike him. I was troubled, and
wondered if he was dealing with a medical problem.

Another hint of trouble ahead came at a meeting of the
Administrative Committee of the General Conference a month or

two later. As Robert Folkenberg opened the committee, he seemed weighed down by a heavy burden. Before we took up the agenda, as usual we sought the Lord's guidance in the deliberations. This morning, as the elder called on me to lead the group in prayer, he informed us that he was dealing with a serious matter of a personal nature that he could not share, and asked me to uphold him before the Lord in the prayer.

Straws in the wind, blowing by, soon forgotten.

But the waters were rising, rising, silently, inexorably.

Suddenly we would find ourselves in the swelling of Jordan.

——————⋅◆⋅——————

The new year was only a few days old when, as I was eating the noon meal in the General Conference cafeteria, I received an urgent message to attend a special meeting. Wondering what was going on, I hurried to the room indicated in the message. Two people were there and waiting for me: attorney Bob Nixon and Bjarne Christensen, chair of the Crisis Management Committee.

They launched immediately into the reason for the urgent meeting. "Listen," they said, "we don't have much time to talk, because we're leaving this afternoon for the PREXAD [President's Executive Council on Administration—the General Conference officer group] meeting in Florida. An item will come up there of possibly grave import for the church. At this point hardly anyone knows about it—not even the General Conference vice presidents. You will need to give careful thought as to how the *Adventist Review* will handle the information that will come to light, so we are giving you a heads-up."

I knew about the PREXAD meeting—nothing unusual in itself. For several years the General Conference officers had convened each January in Florida to discuss major items for the year ahead. I was not an officer, so I did not usually attend.

This year, 1999, the agenda included a matter that Bob and

Bjarne foresaw as having serious consequences. They informed me that although investigation was still proceeding, evidence of such a nature had come to light as to warrant consideration by PREXAD. As they began to tell me about it, I broke in, saying, "I'm not sure I want to hear about this."

"There's more," they replied, "and it gets worse."

The gist of the matter concerned a series of business deals involving General Conference president Robert Folkenberg. Folkenberg had become entangled with one James Moore, not an Adventist, whom the elder had known for a number of years. Moore was a convicted felon who had been incarcerated for fraud 10 years earlier. One of his deals had gone sour. He blamed Folkenberg for his loss and had been threatening a lawsuit for several years.

Folkenberg had attempted to get Moore off his back by making payments to him. Moore wasn't satisfied and eventually went ahead with the lawsuit. He claimed $8 million and named the General Conference, along with Folkenberg and others in the suit.

Moore's claim was lodged in California. When notice of the suit came to the notice of the General Conference, Bob Nixon hired an Adventist trial lawyer in Sacramento, Phil Hiroshima, to represent the church. Hiroshima began to work through the documents in the case. Becoming deeply concerned at what had come to light, he alerted the General Conference legal office.

And so PREXAD would take up the matter. Hiroshima would present the evidence he had found. The elder, who had hired an attorney, would be given opportunity to state his case.

Bob and Bjarne cut short the conversation and hurried to the airport. I went back to the *Review* office, my head spinning. My whole being told me that we were on the brink of developments fraught with peril for the church. The waters of Jordan, now at flood tide, were lapping at our feet.

After mulling over what I had heard, I called the editors together for a closed-door session. I shared the information from Nixon and

Christensen, and also my foreboding that the days just ahead would bring huge pressures to bear on the *Adventist Review* as we endeavored to share with church members news they deserved to hear. There, in that conference room that day, we developed a set of protocols that would guide us in covering the events concerning the General Conference president. We covenanted that our reporting would be accurate, honest, candid, and timely. At the same time we would seek to be redemptive, helping our people to gain a larger perspective on information that was sure to disturb them.

The members of PREXAD returned from Florida, reporting that the Florida meeting had closed early in confusion. When we gathered for the Administrative Committee meeting the following Tuesday morning, it was obvious to me that the elder had lost the committee. Hardly anyone around the table would look at him.

A few days later another meeting of Administrative Committee meeting convened in special session. Chaired by General Conference secretary G. Ralph Thompson, it voted to set up an ad hoc group to investigate the concerns that had come to light and to recommend what course of action, if any, should be pursued. The ad hoc group, 20 in number, was broadly based: three presidents of world divisions, three lay members, one pastor, three women, five General Conference officers, and leaders drawn from church headquarters and the North American Division. Niels-Erik Andreasen, president of Andrews University, was appointed as the chair.

With deep concern I saw my name on the list. It would be the most difficult and painful assignment of my entire work for the church. I would sit in judgment on the conduct of my boss, Pastor Robert S. Folkenberg.

———————————

The dates for the ad hoc group to meet were set for January 25 and 26, 1999. For reasons of confidentiality and travel convenience, the venue would be a motel adjacent to Washington Dulles International Airport in northern Virginia. Immediately following the meeting, on January 27, the Administrative Committee would meet to consider the report and recommendations from the ad hoc group. All the presidents of the world divisions would fly in to take part in the meeting, which would convene at a different location close to Dulles Airport.

By now stories were appearing in the public press about the allegations raised by Moore. Independent Adventist publications had also zeroed in on the matter, and were eagerly following developments to post on their Web sites. In order to ensure that the president received fair and accurate treatment, church leaders took unusual steps to keep the meeting confidential. The hallways of the motel were patrolled by security personnel from the General Conference as well as from the facility. Committee members spent the entire time together in the same room; meals were brought in. When someone needed to visit the restroom, they were escorted by a security officer.

Early on that first day, January 25, a Monday, security found a person, ear to the wall, in the room adjoining the committee venue. He was escorted from the premises.

We gathered that Monday morning with a heavy sense of our painful assignment. After seeking the Lord in prayer, we spent considerable time discussing how we should proceed. In particular, what should be the role of the attorneys? Elder Folkenberg had brought his legal team, which included James Procknow, who had been part of Richard Nixon's defense during his impeachment. The General Conference was represented by some of its legal staff, plus Phil Hiroshima. We eventually reached a consensus that Folkenberg should be present to hear the evidence against him but he would not be permitted to speak during the presentation. Further, Folkenberg and his legal team should withdraw during the following discussion. After this the elder and his team would present their side, with the General Conference attorneys present but not permitted to comment; then they would leave the room as the committee responded to Folkenberg and his attorneys.

Now we turned to consider the evidence gathered by Phil Hiroshima. It was voluminous—more than 20,000 pages of documents. From this mass a selection of key materials had been put together for the ad hoc group to peruse; it ran to 85 pages.

James Moore was involved in multiple companies, some non-profit, some for profit, registered offshore. The relationship between these entities in some instances was unclear: which were real, which were merely "paper" corporations? Moore had spun a large financial web, and Robert Folkenberg, through a long association with Moore, had become entangled in it. In his lawsuit Moore made a series of allegations against Folkenberg, some quite serious, but I do not think that they warrant mention here. Nor do I think it necessary or helpful to go into detail concerning the evidence shared by Hiroshima with the committee. Suffice to say that the materials included trust accounts, offshore dealings, bank accounts, church entities, payments made by Folkenberg to Moore, Folkenberg's relationship and his business ventures to Moore, and hours of recorded telephone conversations. There was also a connection with the Roman Catholic Church. Moore, who had joined that church, claimed to have power of attorney on behalf of the Catholic Church to sue the Seventh-day Adventist Church.

When the elder's turn came to respond, he handed the main presentation to his attorney James Procknow. Now we heard a different interpretation of the same documents the committee had worked through during the morning. Zeroing in point by point on specific areas of concern and questions, Procknow argued that there were no scandalous facts in the documents or on the tapes, there was no theft of church money, no diversion of church money, no violation of the fundamental beliefs of the church so as to warrant discipline, no genuine connection with the Roman Catholic Church, and no personal profit at the expense of the church. Further, Folkenberg's relationship with Moore had involved only a minuscule amount of his time.

The committee then posed questions to the elder directly. This was a painful phase. Folkenberg, who had worked tirelessly as General Conference president, was subjected to kind but penetrating cross-examination by colleagues.

At last the long day came to a close. I went to bed, but slept little. Probably few, if any, of the others who had been in that room slept either. How to put the pieces of the day together? The documentation was clear, but the perceptions of what it meant differed so radically.

I rose early and went for a walk. Although the morning was winter cold, I wanted quiet time to talk with the Lord and try to clear my head. Along the way I met up with Harold Lance, a lay leader of the church and also an attorney. As we discussed the events of the previous day, we agreed that, given the differing interpretations of the data, the ad hoc group would probably conclude that the picture was too clouded to warrant further action by the church.

Gradually, however, the committee moved toward a consensus. Focusing on certain troubling areas, it received more details and called back Elder Folkenberg for further questioning. More and more it became concerned with areas of conflict of interest and misuse of office, as in the president's using his name and influence, as well as General Conference stationery, to promote Moore's business interests. His continuing association and business transactions with James Moore raised questions of judgment and ethics. Thus, when the matter was put to a vote by secret ballot late in the day, an overwhelming majority expressed the conviction that the elder's conduct called for examination by the General Conference Executive Committee.

The next day, Wednesday, January 27, 1999, the Administrative Committee, joined by almost all the presidents from the world divisions, considered the report and recommendations from the ad hoc group. A lengthy discussion followed. By the end of the day the vote carried overwhelmingly: the concerns raised by the elder's conduct were of such a nature as to be brought to the Executive Committee for consideration.

Because the full committee includes all the union presidents—it comprised 268 people—it takes time to call a meeting. Visa and travel arrangements must be processed for members coming from all over the world. Thus, the dates of March 1-7 were set for the critical assembly.

With major events like the crisis of the presidency, inevitably rumors arise and circulate. Some Adventists immediately assumed that the elder was involved in a moral lapse. That was false. On the other side, some saw a "palace coup" to remove him from office. That also was false.

———◆———

Now the *Adventist Review* office faced a test—to get out the news, accurately and fast, as we had pledged ourselves to do. The Administrative Committee action had been taken that Wednesday evening. The next issue would go to press the following Tuesday. Because the *Review* is a weekly, we prepare copy well in advance. Now, however, we decided to scrap the first four pages, including the cover, and substitute the story of grave magnitude. I wanted our coverage to be more than bare facts, so early on Friday morning I wrote a perspective piece, "Caught in the Web," to run with the news.

That same Friday we posted all the copy on the *Adventist Review* Web site. It rolled off the press the following Tuesday. It was a magnificent response on the part of the *Review* staff and the Review and Herald personnel involved.

Yes, we did come under some pressure. The Crisis Management Committee had agreed that it alone would provide the official release of information. We could not confine the *Review*'s coverage to their releases. While the *Review* works closely with the church leaders, it is not a public relations journal. We agreed to share with the committee the copy we had prepared, and invited their input—no more. And we heard from Elder Folkenberg also, expressing his perception that the *Review*'s story was fair overall, but taking exception to the wording in one section.

Having no inkling of what lay ahead, Noelene and I, months before, had planned a visit to our relatives in Australia. With March 1 set as the date for the meeting for the General Conference Executive Committee, we figured we would go ahead and take a two-week vacation.

It became very much a working vacation. Every day I was in touch with the office, following developments and giving instructions. I also sent a long fax message to Elder Folkenberg, in which I expressed some concerns and urged him to consider resigning.

My brother Douglas lived with his wife on Kangaroo Island, an idyllic place offshore from Adelaide. We had reserved a vacation cottage on a quiet bay along from where he lived, but first went to Doug's home. "Someone has been trying to reach you from America," he said, and handed me a name and telephone number. It was Elder Folkenberg; he had tracked me down through the local conference office.

Food was on the table, but I told the others to go ahead without me and called the president. My fax message had impacted him. He wanted to clarify a matter I had raised. And he told me that he had decided to resign the General Conference presidency.

Our cottage on the bay was a Shangri-la. A half mile up from the beach, it looked out on clear, blue water where a few small boats trolled for fish. Few people, no stores.

And no telephone. The only link with the outside world was a lone booth with open sides by the campground at the beach. I figured out the time difference. Emu Bay was 15½ hours ahead of the *Review* office, so in order to catch the editors before they left for home I needed to call before 8:00 a.m. Every morning I walked down the hill, punched in the code, and called the United States. Sometimes the conversations lasted nearly an hour, and I grew cold from the wind whipping off the sea through the open telephone booth.

It was a surreal experience. As I spoke I looked out on the blue waters and tranquillity, while back at the *Review* the General Conference complex was poised, tense, expectant.

On February 8, 1999, Robert Folkenberg called together the staff of the General Conference headquarters to announce that he had resigned the presidency, effective immediately.

Once again, the *Adventist Review* staff sprang into action. Once again, they tore up the issue scheduled for press, inserting new copy in the first four pages.

Noelene and I returned to a strange situation—a twilight-zone phenomena—at world headquarters. Robert Folkenberg had resigned as president, and G. Ralph Thompson was acting president. But Elder Folkenberg still came to the building. He still parked in the slot reserved for the president. He went to his old office and kept posting materials on his personal Web site. The situation was unreal, uncanny. Folkenberg walked the building, greeting the staff. He was no longer the president—or was he?

As March 1 drew on, tension mounted daily, reaching a fever pitch. The Administrative Committee action of January 27 involved less than 50 people. Now the full General Conference Committee of 268 would take up the matter. How would the overseas divisions view the developments that had come about since the beginning of the year? What if a large block of the world church wanted the elder, who was admired and loved, to continue in office? A split, a fracturing of the body, loomed as frightening possibility.

All doors were closed in the packed General Conference auditorium as Pastor G. Ralph Thompson called the extraordinary session to order. The Seventh-day Adventist Church was organized in 1863. In the 136 years since that date no Executive Committee meeting like this one had ever taken place. We faced a new, unwelcome situation, one that our forefathers had not contemplated, one thought so impossible that the church's constitution and policies had no provision in place to deal with it. There was no bylaw, no clause, to guide us for the removal from office of the General Conference president.

We needed divine guidance as never before. Pastor George Brown, retired president of the Inter-American division, led in a devotional study that helped put us in a frame of mind to tackle the issue at hand. Then Pastor Thompson invited Elder Folkenberg to make a statement. He used the opportunity to recount the advances made on his watch—and they were many. Then, at the close, he dropped a bombshell—the lawsuit brought by James Moore had been settled out of court!

The announcement had a palpable effect on the committee, with glad amens sounded by some members. Then Folkenberg left the room.

Thus, when Elder Thompson opened the floor for discussion, immediately some members rose to say that since the lawsuit was no longer an issue, Pastor Folkenberg should continue as General Conference president. Some well-known leaders lent their support to the idea: the committee should vote to refuse to accept Folkenberg's resignation. This was an aspect that many of us had not thought of—the elder's resignation had to be accepted by the Executive Committee before it could become effective.

By this point in the morning it was impossible to predict the outcome of the meeting. Several members had expressed themselves in favor of Folkenberg's continuing as president, but what about the large majority who had remained silent? And what about the General Conference officers—would they be prepared to work again with him, or would we see mass resignations from their positions?

Then Harold Baptiste, secretary of the North American Division, went to the microphone. It would be the most important speech of the day. Calmly he reminded all that, if the committee voted to refuse to accept the elder's resignation, it would not return matters to the previous status. The January 27 action had not called upon the president to resign. Rather, it had called for the full Executive Committee to meet March 1-7 to consider the allegations against him.

Other committee members quickly affirmed Baptiste's comments. Urging members to accept Folkenberg's resignation, they pointed out that the alternative would result in the committee's sitting as a body to consider the full information about the allegations.

As committee members digested these arguments, which correctly stated matters, Robert Folkenberg made a sudden reappearance in the auditorium. After his earlier remarks he had gone to the sound booth, where he had seen and heard all that had transpired. Returning to the microphone, he declared that it was not in his interest or that of the church to continue a lengthy discussion of the matter. In an emotional speech he insisted that even if offered the presidency again, he would decline the opportunity.

Committee members moved quickly to vote on the motion to accept Folkenberg's resignation. The motion passed with near unanimity, and the committee then began selecting persons to lead out in the process for nominating a new president. Soon it was decided that the full General Conference Executive Committee should serve as the Nominating Committee.

By the end of the day the Seventh-day Adventist Church had elected a new president—Pastor Jan Paulsen. And once again the *Adventist Review* editors tore up the cover of the next issue scheduled for the press, replacing 10 pages with a report of the events of the dramatic day and introducing the new leader of the world church.

———◆———

Looking back on those tumultuous days at the start of 1999, I am amazed at the way the Lord brought His church through the crisis. We faced a grave situation—the possible splitting of the world church—and without precedent or constitutional markers to point the way through it. But the Lord, who is the head of the church, guided step by new step until we had crossed Jordan at flood tide.

The General Conference attorneys first became aware of Moore's lawsuit in November 1989. Phil Hiroshima was hired to represent the church and began to investigate Moore's allegations. Only by the turn of the year did his findings begin to circulate among the General Conference leaders. Just two months later the matter had been faced and resolved when, on March 1, 1999, the Seventh-day Adventist Church elected a new president.

The process followed was fair, thorough, businesslike—and speedy. From today's perspective it is hard to see how it could be improved upon. By the time many Adventists began to hear about the lawsuit, the matter was all over. There was no long drawn-out debate, no taking of sides, no draining of energy from mission. The church went on without missing a beat.

Sometimes we complain about the committee structure of the church. We indeed are a church of committees—myriad committees at all levels. We have no pope; we abhor kingly power. We trust the Lord's leading through a multitude of counselors.

This system worked well—very well—for us when the chips were down.

I could write a great deal more on this matter. One day, I expect, it will furnish the material for a doctoral dissertation or a book. But I will simply close with brief mentions of two aspects.

First, before Moore's lawsuit became known and the data began to come to light, a couple of individuals at the General Conference stood tall. With the president, increasingly desperate to break free of Moore's clutches, casting about for a way out, they refused to compromise the conduct of the church's operations. Unbenownst to the rest of us, they took the lonely road of strictly ethical dealings in the face of strong pressures.

Second, the elder at the center of this unique episode in the life of the Adventist Church is not a crook. He displayed poor judgment and, caught in the web that Moore had spun (but which he also had helped form), misused the presidential office in an attempt to get Moore off his back. His story is tragic. So much energy, such creativity, such hard labor to advance the church, such a commanding personality; but ultimately his leadership crashing to ruin because of a long association with a person of dubious character.

I cannot imagine the pain Robert Folkenberg and his dear ones must have endured, still endure. My heart goes out to him and to them. Out of concern for them I wrestled for some time as to whether I could write this book. To try to tell the story of my quarter century in the cockpit of the church and omit this chapter—that would be dishonest. Yet I knew that rehearsing the event, even without going into details, would open up deep wounds. I can only hope that my account will be redemptive for all who read it and especially for the principal players.

I am glad that the story has a happy ending. Elder Folkenberg could have become embittered. He could have united with the critics of the church, put his enormous energy into pulling down the edifice of the church. But instead he chose to work on building it up through the most direct means—evangelism. He devised and organized a program that equips laypeople to go out and preach the Adventist message. It is a big endeavor, now reaching global dimensions. And it has brought large numbers of new members into the church and has revived and nurtured the experience of the thousands of members who have had a part.

I take off my hat to Robert Folkenberg. His work after leaving the General Conference is as fine as anything he accomplished as president.

The final word of praise, however, belongs to our God. He showed Himself to be the Lord of the swelling of Jordan.

CHAPTER 13

Conversations
With Other Churches

"We came together . . . as strangers, we parted . . . as friends."
—From Lutherans and Adventists in Conversation, 1994–1998

An interesting development of the past quarter century has been the increasing frequency of discussions at high level between representatives of the Seventh-day Adventist Church and those of other churches. Most members are hardly aware of these conversations, although the church has not attempted to keep them secret.

This development signals a shift in the way in which others regard Adventists, and we them—and ourselves. For most of our existence we have tended to keep apart from other Christian bodies, ignoring Ellen White's counsel and example. (She featured prominently in the temperance movement in the United States, at times addressing very large gatherings.) At times, because some others scorned or derided us, we lacked the confidence to engage them in an open, frank exchange of beliefs.

Today the Adventist Church increasingly exhibits a healthy self-confidence. From the tiniest of beginnings we have grown under the Lord's good hand into a worldwide denomination that throbs with a sense of purpose and innovation. We count only baptized believers. They number more than 16 million. But in many countries the government census returns show numbers far larger than our official count. It's safe to say that worldwide at least 30 million people identify with the Seventh-day Adventist Church. And beyond the numbers, more and more Adventists have risen like cream to the top in society—presidents and prime ministers, cabinet ministers, famous surgeons, acclaimed musicians. And even to the chaplaincy of the United States Senate.

More and more, Adventists make the news. Occasionally for bad reasons, but usually for good ones. We live longer, have better health. We're part of a church adding a million members annually, doubling every 10 years or so—faster than the Mormons. At a time that the mainline churches are shrinking, Adventists are flourishing.

People want to know what makes us what we are. They want to meet us, to know more about us. Heads of state open their doors to the General Conference president when he goes abroad. And more and more churches are coming to us, wanting to sit down with us and engage in dialogue at the official level.

They have changed. So have we.

Some Adventists get nervous when they learn about any such conversations. They're afraid that we will sell out, compromise our beliefs. Worst of all, that any dialogue will take us down the road to joining the ecumenical movement.

But long ago the apostle Peter admonished Christians of his day, "Always be ready to give a defense to everyone who asks you a reason for the hope that is in you, with meekness and fear" (1 Peter 3:15, NKJV). I believe this counsel applies to us just as much today. If someone or somebody wants to talk, wants to know more about us—our values, our mission, especially our hope—we *must* say yes to the opening. We won't try to figure out their motives—we'll leave that to the Lord—but gladly we'll sit down with them, look them in the eye, and share the Adventist story.

I have been involved in almost all the conversations that have taken place during the past 25 years. Those I missed were because other engagements came in the way of my participation. Up to 2006 I served as a member of the Adventist team; since then I have been the leader. From the beginning of these discussions, Bert B. Beach, the church's world statesperson sine qua non, initiated contacts and chaired from the Adventist side the dialogues. Now, still alert but with advancing years, he takes part as one of the Adventist representatives, but he has handed over the chairing to me.

These many meetings with other Christian leaders have taught me much and enriched me both spiritually and as a person. In these conversations the purpose is to understand and to be understood, and to explore possibilities of cooperation in limited areas such as religious freedom. We sit down, not to debate, not to argue, not to try to one-up the other, but to listen and to share. We mutually seek to shatter misconceptions and stereotypes, so that we can honestly and accurately convey the beliefs of the other.

Honesty is absolutely essential. I learned as an Adventist to be open and forthright, holding nothing back of our doctrines, being ready to admit shortcomings, but also speaking with the conviction that the Lord raised up this movement and that our beliefs can withstand the most searching scrutiny.

Some of these conversations were difficult. Some had moments of high tension. Some were pure delight. But in all I saw the Lord's good hand upon us and over us. And I made dear new friends from unexpected quarters.

⸻

My first experience of dialogues with representatives of other churches came in the late 1980s. A group of leading evangelical scholars, led by Kenneth Kantzer, at that time editor of *Christianity Today*, wanted to know how they should relate to Seventh-day Adventists.

Just how the meeting came about I do not know; nor was it ever publicized. By mutual agreement both parties decided to keep private the meeting and its conclusions. Again, I can only speculate as to the reasons. All the subsequent conversations of which I was a part were shared with the church. For the more significant ones, I wrote a page or so in the *Adventist Review*. Back in the 1980s many evangelicals were suspicious of Adventists, and some were hostile. Thirty years earlier Walter Martin and Donald Barnhouse, editor of *Eternity* magazine, had met with several General Conference representatives and concluded that Adventists should be considered not members of a cult but genuine Christians. When Martin and Barnhouse published their findings, a storm broke out in the evangelical world, with thousands canceling their subscriptions to *Eternity*. Perhaps in the 1980s Kantzer and his colleagues were wary of a repeat performance.

On the Adventist side, the conversations with evangelicals in the 1950s had resulted in debate and dispute over the book *Questions on Doctrine* that summarized the positions taken by the Adventist representatives. While the book, which circulated widely throughout the church, had general acceptance, a vociferous minority saw in it evidence that those who represented the church in the conversations had watered down our doctrines in order to curry favor with the evangelicals. Thus, when the new meeting was planned, I expect Adventist leaders likewise were happy to keep it under wraps to forestall another round of accusations.

For many years I have been interested—and puzzled—concerning the evangelical reaction to Adventism. The evangelicals are not a separate denomination. Rather, they are drawn from many denominations on the basis of shared convictions concerning the inspiration of the Scriptures, the Incarnation, virgin birth, atoning death, and resurrection of Jesus, the Second Coming, evangelism, the new birth, and the life of piety manifested in prayer, Bible study, and Christian witness. All these beliefs and practices are ones to which Adventists heartily ascribe: we are more evangelical than the evangelicals. (Belief in immortality of the soul and eternal hell were previously hallmarks of evangelical thought, but that is no longer the case.)

But instead of embracing Adventists as brothers and sisters in Christ, many evangelicals held Adventists at arm's length. Some denounced us savagely as followers of a sect or a cult. Others held ambivalent feelings. While attitudes have softened during the past few decades, the strongest attacks against Adventist still arise from many evangelical Christians.

The conversations in which I participated in the late 1980s were not a dialogue. They were a one-way street. Kantzer and friends came to investigate Adventists; we did not investigate them. Their approach was to work through the fundamental beliefs, which at that time numbered 27. The Adventist team was headed by Bert Beach and included George Reid, Gerhard Hasel, William Shea, and me. We met for two days at General Conference headquarters, which was then still in Takoma Park, Maryland.

Kantzer and his associates quickly decided on two articles from the fundamental beliefs that raised flags: number 17, dealing with Ellen White and the gift of prophecy, and number 23, on the ministry of Jesus in the heavenly sanctuary. They analyzed these articles word by word, phrase by phrase, checking and probing to be sure they understood our positions accurately. On Ellen White they zeroed in on the relation of her writings to Scripture. Since Adventists believe she had the prophetic gift, do we put her writings on the same level as the Bible? Our answer (which was hers in her day) was no. The Scriptures are the test of all other writings, including hers.

The article on 1844 and the investigative judgment took much longer to explain. Here the key issue involved the gospel. Did our unique doctrine run counter to the all-sufficient sacrifice of Christ on Calvary and thereby negate assurance of salvation in Him? The careful wording of the article—that the pre-Advent judgment *reveals* who are *in Christ*, rather than declaring a decision based on human effort—convinced the visiting scholars that this Adventist doctrine, so often misunderstood and castigated, does not negate the gospel.

At the close of the two days of courteous but intense discussion, our visitors declared that the time together had made clear to them that Seventh-day Adventist are indeed evangelical Christians. I would love to have shared that conclusion with readers of the *Adventist Review*.

I would love even more to have passed on a comment made by Kenneth Kantzer toward the close of the conversation. We had been explaining our understanding of the remnant, and looking at the great prophecy of Revelation 12-14, with its listing of the commandments of God as designating God's true followers in the end-time (Rev. 12:17; 14:12). After we had finished our presentation, Kantzer said, "Never give up your Sabbath! You Adventists are an example to us evangelicals. We are weak in obedience—you are an example to us" (the words are mine, but the thought was his). I have often recalled that dramatic moment, when this gracious Christian gentleman spoke from the heart a profound insight.

At last, after more than 20 years, I am sharing his words and the meeting itself. In doing so, I do not see any abrogation of confidentiality. Whatever reasons were advanced back then to keep the conversations under wraps, they can no longer apply. The world has moved on, and so have both the Adventist Church and the evangelical movement. It is time to unlock the story of the past.

***

Because news of the Kantzer meeting was never made public, it is impossible to gauge the effects of the discussions. Doubtless the Adventist Church benefited from having its beliefs accurately understood by influential evangelical figures. With one major dialogue, however, the results were major and immediate.

In 1994 the Seventh-day Adventist Church commenced an official conversation with the Lutheran World Federation. Once again Bert Beach, through the high regard in which he was held among world Christian leaders, played a major role in bringing the event about.

For Adventists, the stakes were high. Many of our people who live in countries in which the state supports the Lutheran Church suffered from a low self-esteem. The press frequently referred to their church as a cult or sect. Often they worshipped in unobtrusive chapels on side streets, with small notices announcing their presence. I know this from experience, having to search hard to locate the Adventist congregation for a Sabbath preaching appointment. They avoided the designation *kirke* (church); instead, they labeled themselves the *Adventgemeinde* (Adventist community). If the Lutheran Church, the official church of the state, could recognize and acknowledge that Adventists are genuine Christians, that could mean much for our members.

For the initial round of discussions, the Adventists offered to serve as hosts. We gathered at our school in Marienhohe, near Darmstadt in Germany, setting aside the entire week. This exploratory session would determine whether we found sufficient elements in common to justify extending the conversation into the future.

The Lutheran World Federation, based in Geneva, Switzerland, represents about 60 million Lutherans. To meet with the Adventists, its leaders selected a truly international team. Its members came from Germany, Scandinavia, Africa, South America, Canada, and the United States. By contrast, most of the Adventist group came from the United States, although in terms of our roots we were every bit as diverse as the Lutherans.

Cochairs for the conversation were Bert Beach and Ole Kvarme, a kindly Norwegian bishop who was acquainted with Adventists. As we met around the table and spent time in personal introductions, however, the atmosphere was decidedly icy. By body language and even words, several members of the Lutheran delegation conveyed the low opinion they had of Adventists. They thought we were a simplistic, unlearned sect that did not merit their time. One German pastor, as he introduced himself, went so far as to say, "I don't know why I am here today. I only came because my church told me I should come."

As the day wore on, the dynamic changed noticeably. The Lutherans were surprised at the high regard in which the Adventists held Martin Luther—as a person raised up by God, almost a hero. Suspicious that we were piling on praise in an effort to impress them, they queried us further. Of course, our words were totally sincere, and at last the Lutherans accepted them as such.

An even more dramatic moment came when the freewheeling discussion moved to Adventists' understanding of the gospel. One of the members of our team, Hans Heinz from Germany, was a Luther scholar who had written his doctoral dissertation on Luther and the gospel. With amazement the Lutherans heard him quote Luther at length, verbatim, in German. You could almost see the misconceptions of Adventists (as naive and ignorant in theological matters) disappearing like a morning mist.

We began each day's meeting with a devotional time, Lutherans and Adventists alternating in planning and leading the worship. As we sang and prayed together to the one God, Father of the Lord Jesus Christ, and as we shared passages of Scripture precious in our heritage, we began to bond in faith and love.

That week we spent a lot of time together, seeking to understand each other's beliefs but also one another as persons. We took all our meals together. We went on walks by twos or threes. By Friday of that week it was obvious to all from both sides that we should plan for an extended dialogue. We figured that three more rounds were necessary for fruitful work—on the gospel, including the law and the Sabbath; on the church and sacraments; and on eschatology. We agreed to recommend this to the respective bodies that had authorized the initial discussion: the Administrative Committee of the General Conference, and the Lutheran World Federation.

Our first conversation formally ended that Friday, but the members of the Lutheran delegation had planned to stay on in Germany for some days. We invited them to join us for Sabbath services, and they agreed. They went to Sabbath school, participating in a study of the lesson, then stayed on for divine worship. That day the Adventist pastor preached a fine Bible-based sermon, and our guests expressed appreciation of it.

It was the climax of a week that began unpromisingly but closed full of good things. These Lutherans, drawn from far and wide, had encountered our knowledge of the Bible and of history. They had experienced our worship. Most of all, they had come to know and appreciate us as men and women who loved the Lord and trusted Him for our salvation. They went their various ways enlightened, looking forward to our next meeting together.

Both authorizing bodies, after receiving the respective reports and recommendations for further discussions, gave the green light.

We came together again in 1996, at a Lutheran retreat center in Mississauga, near Toronto, Canada. Scholarly papers on justification by faith, the law, and law and gospel were presented from each side, with vigorous discussion. The Lutheran representatives probed the Adventist papers, wanting to be clear as to where we stood vis-à-vis the gospel. By the end of the week they were satisfied that Adventists truly believe in *sola fides* and *sola gracias* (by faith alone, by grace alone), as well as in *sola scriptura* (the Bible alone). It was a turning point. With this recognition they were more ready to accept whatever differences in doctrine might emerge in subsequent discussions.

Adventists hosted the next year's conversation (in 1997), and we selected a Christian retreat center, simple in amenities but picturesque in setting, in the hills above Geneva, Switzerland. The focus this time was on ecclesiology and the understanding of church authority. As before, background papers provided the framework for extensive discussions.

The final consultation convened in 1998 in Cartigny, Switzerland. It took up the area we had the least in common—eschatology. At times the discussion became animated, as the Lutherans quizzed our views on Babylon, the remnant, and the mark of the beast. We held nothing back. Courteously but clearly we shared our convictions, arguing our positions from Scripture. Some of our ideas were indeed hard for the Lutherans to swallow, and at one point I wondered if the dialogue would break up. But we had come far since that first meeting in Darmstadt in 1994. We had come to appreciate and even love each other. We had become friends.

For Lutherans, the prophetic portions of the Bible are almost completely a blank. For Adventists, they course in the veins. I remember well a comment from one of the Lutherans during this final round at Cartigny: "We Lutherans don't have enough eschatology; you Adventists have too much!"

At each of the last three sessions, a common statement, based on the background papers and discussions, was drafted and approved. It fell to Risto Saarinen, a fine Finnish scholar, and me to do the legwork for the statement—which entailed late nights. We worked closely together to prepare a draft, which had to go to each delegation for discussion and fine-tuning, then to the combined group for final approval. Before the last session, a small drafting group met for two days at General Conference headquarters in Silver Spring, Maryland.

The final conversation, at Cartigny, completed work on the common statement and made recommendations for the future life of our respective churches. This meeting was also visited by General Conference president Robert S. Folkenberg and the general secretary for the Lutheran World Federation, Ishmael Noko.

Once again we closed with a worship service. We traveled by hired buses to the Adventist college at Collonges, France, and celebrated the Sabbath together. The church calendar called for the Communion service, and our Lutheran friends willingly entered into it. As a Canadian Lutheran and I shared the basin and the towel, tears rolled down his cheeks.

All the papers of our time together, 1994-1998, were gathered up and, along with the report and recommendations, jointly published in a book, *Lutherans and Adventists in Conversation.*

The report and recommendations run to 18 papers. It contains the following paragraph, which captures the spirit and work of the dialogue:

"We came together in 1994 as strangers, we parted in 1998 as friends. We came with questions, we parted with mutual appreciation. While significant doctrinal differences remain, we found much in common: a love for the Word of God, a shared heritage from the Reformation, a deep appreciation for the work and teachings of Martin Luther, a concern for religious freedom, and above all, the gospel of justification by grace through faith alone. By spending many hours together listening and seeking to understand, agreeing and disagreeing, eating and especially praying, we experienced the bonding of the Spirit under our one Lord Jesus Christ. Each of us who was given the opportunity to be part of these common conversations feels enriched intellectually and spiritually by this adventure of faith, and we give thanks to our God from whom all blessings flow."

Among the recommendations one finds this: "We recommend that Lutherans in their national and regional church contexts do not treat the Seventh-day Adventist Church as a sect but as a free church and a Christian world communion." This was a huge development for the life of the Adventist people in Europe. I praise the Lord for what this conversation—the longest and most important—accomplished.

Over the course of the years I was involved in several other interchurch dialogues. Some were of short duration with lesser-known entities, like the Church of God (Seventh Day) or the Assemblies of Yahweh. Others involved well-recognized denominations and lasted longer.

I found myself once again in Switzerland, at a retreat center in the beautiful hills above Lake Geneva, for a week of dialogue. Adventists and representatives of the World Alliance of Reformed Churches—churches whose heritage goes back to the Reformers John Calvin and John Knox—sat down together and explored areas of common ground and differences. This conversation, however, did not have a life beyond the initial meeting: the Reformed group was much more interested in exploring cooperation in areas of social justice than in discussing theology. We Adventists are leery of getting involved in "causes."

The most delightful dialogue in all my experience was with the Salvation Army. This world communion, whose work for the poor Ellen White commended, has much in common with the Seventh-day Adventist Church. Both arose around the same time. Both involved married partners in their founding (William and Catherine Booth, and James and Ellen White). And both have roots that reach back into the Wesleyan revival.

As we met together over three rounds of conversations, the devotional periods were especially inspiring. We sang the same hymns, we used the same language in prayer, and we had the same straightforward approach to the Word of God. Although there are significant differences in doctrinal understanding—notably concerning the Sabbath, Ellen White's role and writings, and the heavenly sanctuary—we enjoyed warm fellowship as brothers and sisters in Christ.

A dialogue of a very different nature brought the wheel full circle. I started with the unreported meeting of Adventists and evangelicals in the 1980s. Some 20 years later the Seventh-day Adventist Church engaged in conversation with delegates from the World Evangelical Alliance, which claims to represent about 420 million evangelicals. The discussions, which took place over two years, were intense and at times tense.

The possibility of convening the conversations had been mentioned informally over several years. By the time they eventually got off the ground, personnel had changed, leading perhaps to a lack of clarity as to the purpose of the discussions. We Adventists prepared careful, biblically reasoned papers for each of the meetings, which were hosted first by the evangelicals at the Baptist seminary in Prague, Czech Republic, and the next year by the Adventists at Andrews University. But on neither occasion did the other side come with corresponding presentations.

Thus, instead of a dialogue, the Adventists found themselves placed in the role of defenders of their beliefs. It was a skewed situation that we had not anticipated. Further, some of those from the evangelical group, while friendly, manifested a sharply critical attitude toward our doctrines. One teacher sat silently day by day, two larger folders by his side on the table. Toward the close of the week (this was in the first session) he revealed the contents of the folders—attacks on Ellen White that he had assembled from the Internet!

When we met the second year, the papers (all from the Adventist side) focused on Adventists' distinctive doctrines—the Sabbath, Ellen White, and the heavenly sanctuary. Although in both presentation and discussion the Adventists reasoned from the Scriptures, the evangelicals were convinced that we based our positions on Ellen White's writings instead of the Bible. Even after we traced the history of how these doctrines came to be part of who we are, the other side seemed hardly moved. Thus, as we began to shape a joint statement to conclude the conversation, the draft they initially proposed stated that Adventists relied on sources other than Scripture for their distinctive teachings! That, of course, was totally unacceptable to us. We countered that if they insisted on such a view, we would demand that the final statement also include the position that Sunday observance was based on sources other than the Bible.

With this the evangelicals backed off, and we were able eventually to arrive at a statement we could all assent to. It set forth areas of agreement, but in a longer section the areas of disagreement. Finally, it pointed to areas of possible cooperation in specific areas, such as religious liberty and help for the needy in society.

It was a satisfactory—and satisfying—conclusion to what had been a difficult process.

I feel confident that these conversations with other churches have been of significant benefit to Seventh-day Adventists. Others have come to see us as we are, without the distortions and stereotypes that led us to be dubbed a sect or a cult. And we ourselves have become less exclusive, more open to acknowledge that the Lord uses many agencies to accomplish His work on earth.

On a personal level, they broadened and enriched my thinking. They also at times deepened my spiritual life as I encountered men and women of deep piety whose tradition differs greatly from mine.

These conversations inevitably brought letters to the office calling for a reply. Some Adventists were suspicious, certain that nothing good could come of meeting with others, that it was all a waste of time and money. It didn't help that sometimes, as representatives of the other side reported or were interviewed regarding a just-completed dialogue, they put their own ecumenical "spin" on what had happened. The media at times played up a minor aspect of such reports, leading to misunderstandings.

I found that the best way to handle Adventist misgivings was to share the joint statements and papers we presented. During the long conversation with the Lutherans one independent group issued dire warnings about what was going on. When the report and papers were made public, they hadn't a word to say.

It's still the best way. Truth can stand investigation. And the truth is still the best answer.

CHAPTER 14

Reinventing the *Review*

If you can keep your head when all about you
Are losing theirs and blaming it on you;
If you can trust yourself when all men doubt you,
But make allowance . . . too; . . .
If you can meet with Triumph and Disaster
And treat those two imposters just the same; . . .
Yours is the Earth and everything that's in it.
—Rudyard Kipling

I had worked for the church 23 years to the day when I took over the *Adventist Review* as editor in chief. During that period every three years, on average, I had a change in responsibilities, either in location or job description. In a manner of which I was not aware, the Lord, I believe, was exposing me to new situations and new challenges that would help prepare me for what would be the summit of my service.

When I retired on December 31, 2006, I was still editor in chief of the *Adventist Review*. After the previous 23 years of frequent changes, I had been in one post, unchanged, for 24 years and one month.

Yet the long haul was one of change also. When I left the *Review* office, I was not only editor of the *Review*. I was also executive publisher of the church paper, as well as editor in chief and executive publisher of a new magazine, *Adventist World*. Much had changed in structures—not in mission, but in ways to accomplish the mission.

Furthermore, much had changed with the *Review* itself. I was blessed with fine editorial teams over the years, and we were constantly reinventing the church paper. Every three years or so (that is how it came out; we did not follow a fixed pattern for change) we fine-tuned the magazine, adjusting design, content, or marketing strategy. Some of the changes were major, repositioning the paper and giving it a new look. We sought to keep the *Review* fresh and up-to-date.

I shall not attempt to chronicle all the ways in which we tried to reinvent the *Review*. Let me give a bird's-eye view of these 24 exciting years—years that entailed slogging in the trenches, meeting deadlines, and safeguarding the content for nearly 1,300 issues, but years rich in creativity and fulfillment. I look back over the time and recall words that described the way the French Revolution appeared to its enthusiasts at its commencement:

"Bliss was it in that dawn to be alive,

But to be young was very heaven!" (William Wordsworth).

The plan to bring the *Adventist Review* under the General Conference involved some controversy. When the plan was brought to the 1982 Spring Meeting, several committee members expressed serious reservations. "The *Review* may become a *Pravda!*" protested one speaker, reflecting his opinion of that paper, which at that time towed the Communist party line.

That same meeting confirmed me as editor-elect of the *Review*. Along with the other editors, I supported the proposal for the church paper to stay at church headquarters when the Review and Herald Publishing Association completed its move to Hagerstown, Maryland, by the close of the year. I felt strongly that in order to keep their fingers on the pulse of the church, the editors needed to be where the action is.

The Spring Meeting voted the change, which made the General Conference the publisher (that is, the legal owner) of the

Adventist Review and its editors part of the General Conference staff. Subsequent events have confirmed that the decision was a wise one. At no time did I feel pressure from the General Conference leadership to make the church paper the mouthpiece for the administration. I enjoyed a close, respectful relationship with each of three presidents who were my bosses—a relationship that I don't think could have been possible had the editors been separated by 75 miles.

For the publishing house, however, the change was a bitter pill to swallow. The *Review* was the house's flagship journal. It had existed before the publishing house began. It gave its name to the publishing house. When the house drew up plans for its large new facility in Hagerstown, it allotted to the *Adventist Review* editors a suite of choice corner offices with a magnificent view of the campus. For several months those offices remained empty in the new facility, as the publishing house administration hoped against hope that the decision taken by the Spring Meeting would be reversed. To them it was unthinkable that the editors of the *Review*, which the house continued to print, should be located elsewhere.

Just before the publishing house moved out of Washington, the president of the company asked me to meet with him. When I arrived at his office, I found all his officers gathered with him. They greeted me cordially and then launched into an orchestrated presentation as to why it would be impossible to get out the *Review* if the editors didn't move to Hagerstown. They made a powerful presentation.

I was a rookie, just taking over the paper, and surrounded by people of a different mind. But I had done my homework and thought the matter through. When they at last completed the presentation and waited for my response, I said, "Gentlemen, I'm disappointed in you." They were shocked. I paused and went on. "Here you are, building this state-of-the-art new publishing house, and you're telling me that you can't do what other publishers already are doing? Look at *Time, Newsweek,* or any of the other magazines.

Their editors are located in one place, but they print elsewhere. How are they able to do that? I'm disappointed in you."

Taken aback, they demanded, "How do you intend to coordinate the work?"

"Easy—by fax and by courier. We can fax pages back and forth. One of the editors will drive up to Hagerstown for one day each week."

End of meeting. And that's how we got the *Review* out each week without missing a beat. Our editorial office had the first fax machine in the General Conference. Before long, other departments wanted to use it; then they bought their own. Later, of course, the computer age took over.

———◆———

The "divorce" of the *Adventist Review* from the Review and Herald was a messy one. Not in relationships—they remained fine. I had high regard for the people who copyedited, proofread, designed, and ran the presses. They worked hard and well, with pride in their work. But the business side of the arrangement left much to be desired. Although the General Conference as publisher was legally the owner, it left the money side with the house. The house received all the revenues from subscriptions and advertising, returning to the General Conference Treasury each month a sum that had been negotiated prior to the split. Salaries of the editors and office operating expenses all came from the General Conference.

It was (and is!) an arrangement that left much to be desired. Inevitably, misunderstandings arose from time to time. For instance, when house management decided to raise the subscription price, as they did from time to time, I had no idea whether the increase was justified or not, since I was shut out of the finances of the paper. The interests of the house and the interests of the editors were parallel but not identical. For the house, the bottom line was profit; for the editors, the bottom line was circulation. We knew that every time the price went up we lost readers, and that bothered us. No doubt it bothered the house some, but not as much as it bothered us, because the *Review* remained profitable.

Under the terms of the joint arrangement, virtually the entire operation of the *Adventist Review*—everything except the editing—remained the responsibility of the house. The marketing area in particular caused me many sleepless nights.

My biggest headache—one that was with me from the first day until the last—was the decline in circulation. The circulation peaked at 96,000 in 1963, and it has slowly declined ever since. By the time I took over it was down to about 70,000. Many factors were at work: changes in reading habits (people watching TV and reading less), union papers expanding in size and content, new magazines in the independent press, and so on. We conducted periodic surveys of readers and nonreaders. Again and again the results came in the same—subscribers wanted the *Review* to continue as a weekly; nonsubscribers wanted it less frequently.

Shortly after becoming editor, I used to say that I'd sleep well at night only when the circulation hit 100,000. How hard we tried—tried for all 24 years—to build it up.

But it slowly continued to erode.

The marketing was in the hands of the Review and Herald. They valued the *Adventist Review*—it made a good profit—but it was only one of a dozen or so periodicals they were trying to build up. Back at the editorial office, we had plenty to do without getting into marketing, but we had ideas to make the paper go—plenty of ideas. We'd present our ideas (some wild, some worth a try) to the Review and Heralds representatives, but nothing ever came of them.

And the circulation kept slowing falling.

We had set up an advisory council for the *Adventist Review*. Made up of church leaders and laypeople with a keen interest in the *Review*, they met once a year and brainstormed. They too were troubled about the falling circulation, and would demand of me, "What are you doing about it?"

I was placed in an impossible situation—called to account for something that I had no hand in. It bothered me enormously, and I chafed under it.

Over the years we made many changes, introduced innovations, tried new products connected with the *Adventist Review*. All—every one of them, no exception—were driven by the passion to reverse the decline in circulation.

———◆———

During the 1980s the North American Division, which had been administered by the General Conference, began a process of separation that eventually led to its taking responsibility for its own operation. As the newly emergent entity stretched its wings, it made several changes in the publications that served the needs of its members. A new Sabbath school lesson plan, *Collegiate Quarterly*, was developed; *College People*, a new magazine for young adults, appeared; and *Insight*, the existing youth periodical, was refocused to appeal to a teenage readership.

Now the idea of a North American Division publication became advocated. The new division needed its own church paper, it was argued; the *Adventist Review* was a General Conference, not a North American Division, journal.

I became concerned about the impact of such a church paper on the *Review*. Throughout its long history its readership had been overwhelmingly based in North America, and that is still the case. A new church paper for the division would set up a competitive situation that, I believed, would not be in the best interests of the division or the General Conference.

In 1985 I went to see Elder Charles Bradford, the president of the North American Division. We were good friends. I had several times sought his kind, wise counsel. "Brad," I told him, "my staff and I are ready to serve the needs of the division. If you wish, we will take one of our issues each month and shape it to serve the church in North America. The *Review* has a name that is widely known and accepted, so the people will receive it well. And you won't need to set up a new editorial office and staff."

Elder Bradford considered the idea and soon issued a directive. There would be no new church paper set up for North America. Instead, the division would work with the *Adventist Review* to meet its publishing needs.

I consider this development to be one of the major achievements that took place on my watch.

Now, a further decision: the NAD edition of the *Adventist Review* should be provided without charge to the homes of all members. Funding would come from a sharing arrangement, with the General Conference, division, union conferences, and conferences each paying a portion. The plan would be tried for three years and then reviewed.

Participation by each unit was voluntary. With so many entities involved, there was much work to be done to try to get everyone on board. Elder Bradford gave a strong lead, and other members of his team threw their weight behind the plan. I also spent much time meeting with union committees, explaining the proposal and answering questions.

By the end of 1985 all the union conferences had signed on, and almost all the conferences. With the dawn of the new year, the first issue of *Adventist Review,* NAD edition rolled off the press and was mailed to almost every Adventist home in the United States, Canada, and Bermuda.

After three years the North American Division leadership, along with the union presidents, voted to continue the plan on an annual basis. Eventually they decided that it should be made ongoing without periodic review. It has been in place without change since 1986.

But that first issue of 1986 marked another big change: the *Review* itself was reinvented. During the previous year the editors spent many hours in discussion and brainstorming with personnel from the Review and Herald, critically assessing the paper's strengths, weaknesses, opportunities, and threats. Together we decided that the new *Review* should be positioned to appeal to a younger readership. That meant a new design and new features, with a dropping of some aspects from the past.

The new *Review* came with a racy, dynamic design that signaled a radical break. It carried the tagline "Weekly News and Inspiration for Seventh-day Adventists," and it dropped the old Back Page that for years had carried short news items. It also introduced two pages of late-breaking news early in the magazine as Newsbreak.

Response to the changes poured in. I was amazed at the way in which the new *Review* was perceived. "If the *Review* can change, the church can change" was the refrain commonly sounded. The timing was right, in the Lord's providence, I believe. After the down years of the early 1980s—years of negativity, of criticism of the church and its leaders—Adventists were ready to welcome a fresh new day.

In the period before 1986, some General Conference leaders had argued that if nonsubscribing members (the great majority) could only get a glimpse of what they were missing, they would want to buy the *Review* to have it in their home every week. Thus, these leaders lent their voices in advocating the idea of what became known as the NAD edition. And for a while their opinion seemed to be borne out by events: orders for new subscriptions poured into the Review and Herald. My personal goal of a 100,000 subscription base began to appear realistic.

These were heady, exciting days. I look back on them as a time of infectious creativity, as week by week the editors worked together to come up with ever-fresh ideas to push the church paper forward.

From my vantage point today, the design of the 1986 new *Review* looks anything but attractive. The cover was not such as to wear well—and we in fact abandoned it after about four years. Throughout the magazine the eye met rules everywhere, rules upon rules! They conveyed energy but lacked grace. Still, the new design was right in one big respect—it forced the reader to recognize that the *Review* had been reinvented.

I have one regret concerning the 1986 *Review*. For a while subscriptions surged, but slowly they tapered off. Eventually they reverted to the old pattern of slow erosion of the base, until the figure was lower than it had been in 1985. Then more and more we heard a new reason given for not subscribing to the weekly: we get it once a month free, and that's all we need. And that reason is still very much an obstacle to the marketing of the *Review*. But the regret is this. During those heady months of 1986 when the new subs poured in and we editors poured creativity into the magazine, did we push the envelope too far? Did we get out too far in front of our loyal subscriber base? I have no way of knowing, but my gut suspicion is that we may have.

For several years the *Adventist Review* expanded into video production. It was an area that opened to us as an opportunity rather than something we sought. Wanting to position the *Review* as up-to-date and increase its appeal to younger Adventists, I grasped the opportunity. The other editors, already fully loaded with preparing a new issue every week, had some doubts about the extra work entailed, but since for the most part the burden fell on me, they assented to the enlargement of the *Review*'s mission.

The first video edition of the *Review* was shot in Rio de Janeiro, at the conclusion of the 1986 Annual Council that was held in that city. I can hardly believe our naïveté. We filmed live in the lobby of the council hotel, without script or teleprompter, as the clock wound down for us to leave for the airport.

Kind people said nice things about our "Report From Rio," but in reality it was terrible. Maybe OK as comedy: legs spread apart, wide-eyed faces staring into the camera, fumbling and faltering.

Two years later the church asked us to try our hands again. The Annual Council was to convene in Nairobi, Kenya, and General Conference president Neal Wilson felt the time had come to prepare a video on Adventists in Africa, where new members were flocking into the church.

This time plans and preparations were vastly superior to the 1986 effort. Two pros in video production—David Brillhart and Ray Tetz—sat down with me and laid out protocols for the film on Africa. It would seek to be a high-class production that left the viewer with images and sounds that accurately portrayed the church in Africa. We would avoid the stereotypes of poverty, witch doctors, and ignorance. Instead, the film would be one (the first one!) that would make Africans themselves feel proud.

Two camera crews went to work, one in West Africa, the other in East Africa. They captured hundreds of hours of high-quality footage; they captured the spirit of the church in Africa. I joined them in East Africa (after climbing Mount Kilimanjaro with Elder Wilson and four others) and hosted the video. After editing, it emerged as a 60-minute film in magazine format with four segments, titled *Africa: Continent of Explosive Growth*.

The firm garnered an award for excellence in media. It circulated widely.

And Africans were proud of the way it portrayed their homeland.

Brillhart, Tetz, and I became associated in more video projects. I enjoyed their company. They were young, full of ideas, demanded excellence of themselves and others, and wanted to put their considerable talents to use of the church. At that time both were employed at the General Conference, though later both branched out on their own and became successful media producers and consultants.

We came up with the idea of an online report of each day's

events for the approaching 1990 General Conference session in Indianapolis. The *Adventist Review*, as it had done for many years, prepared daily print *Bulletins*. Why not daily video counterparts?

It was, perhaps, the craziest idea I ever agreed to. Already we at the *Review* worked day and night on the *Bulletins*—the church paper in effect functioned like a newspaper—so why add to the load? But we did. *On Line Edition* ran for 30 minutes each evening of the session.

That session elected a new president, Robert S. Folkenberg, high-energy and media-savvy. Now we three got the idea of a quarterly video magazine for churches to show on Sabbath morning worship services. We drew up a proposal and presented it to the chief. Before we knew it, he had taken it to the Annual Council leaders, and they had endorsed it and given approval for funding. It was now October; the president wanted the plan to go into effect in January! This would all be in addition to the other responsibilities each of us carried.

Thus was born *On Line Edition,* a 60-minute video program that was mailed out to the churches each quarter. It consisted of a theme segment, a newscast, a mission segment, and a fourth segment of varying content. For the first *On Line* we selected the theme of the Second Coming, and traveled from east to west and north to south interviewing Adventists about "the blessed hope." The result was an upbeat, exhilarating program that viewers loved. We titled that edition "People of Hope," a phrase that continues to have life among Seventh-day Adventists.

On Line Edition ran for slightly more than two years. The number of churches requesting the quarterly video grew steadily and passed 4,000. We varied the theme and spared no effort to keep the program appealing: for a theme on righteousness by faith we traveled to London, England, for the story of John Wesley's conversion.

On Line Edition was successful, but getting it out was killing us—at least it was killing me. When in 1993 the North American

Division decided to move to satellite programming, it was time to let it go. On several counts it was time to move on.

———◆———

The 1990s brought several changes that impacted the *Adventist Review* office: in the introduction of cost centers at the General Conference, and clarification of the relationship of the *Adventist Review* to the Review and Herald.

With the Adventist Church growing rapidly outside North America, the overseas fields put ever-increasing pressure on top church leadership to downsize the headquarters operation and free up additional funds for the world church. Now some departmental staff who had been elected at the 1990 session to serve a five-year term suddenly found themselves out of a job. It was a time of uncertainty that affected employee morale.

As administrator of the *Review* office, I felt the pressure keenly. The *Review* staff, while not excessive for the work we had to do, was larger than that of most departments. Further, the Review and Herald's periodic disbursement from the revenues it received from the church paper covered the salaries of about four editors. Nevertheless, at a time of downsizing, our office came under close scrutiny from which we barely emerged unscathed.

At this time the Treasury also set up cost centers for each unit on its payroll. Along with the rest of the General Conference, the *Adventist Review* office was held to a tight, line-item budget that left almost no wiggle room for new initiatives. With these changes, financial management became an added burden that caused me considerable stress.

From this point on I became drawn into financial considerations that I had not anticipated and for which I was not naturally inclined. I felt strongly that the church paper needed to continually explore new ways to keep fresh. But new initiatives meant funding—which was not available from the General Conference Treasury. The only way was to find new sources of funding. Thus, over the succeeding years I found myself in a role that would have seemed unthinkable during my days in academia—fund-raising. I didn't like it, but I did it because I wanted the *Review* to go ahead.

Under the Folkenberg presidency, with its passion and drive for greater efficiency in General Conference operations, the murky relationship of the *Adventist Review* and the publishing house came up for examination. For years I'd been frustrated by the lack of clarity in the arrangement worked out in 1982. I think, also, that it was not in the best interests of either the *Review* or the Review and Herald.

The two possible solutions to the situation were to return the ownership of the *Adventist Review* to the Review and Herald Publishing Association or for the General Conference, as owner, to take over the total management. The latter, however, would entail the General Conference Treasury getting involved in running a business, which they did not wish to get into. But neither was the General Conference ready to relinquish its role as publisher of the church's leading journal.

After considerable discussions, the decision was made to maintain the basic relationship of shared responsibility, but to modify it so that the General Conference as owner could exercise greater control. An *Adventist Review* Publishing Board, with the president as chair and the editor as secretary, was put in place to give overall guidance for the total operation.

The first action of the new board, which had its initial meeting in December 1995, was to appoint me as executive publisher of the *Adventist Review*. I was now, in addition to the existing editorial responsibility, to represent the interest of the General Conference in all aspects of the operation of the church paper. At the next meeting of the Review and Herald board, of which I was a member, I brought this change to the attention of members. I wanted the minutes to record that the new responsibilities as executive publisher created a potential conflict of interest.

Little did I realize that the days ahead would indeed bring a sharp and painful conflict, and that I would be at the center of it.

Other significant changes came with the General Conference exerting its publisher role. While finances of the *Adventist Review* operation basically remained with the publishing house, they were spelled out by an annual contract. Further, the house assigned a full-time salary for a person to market the Review. This person, nevertheless, reported to the executive publisher.

From my perspective, these changes marked a big improvement. The house-*Review* relationship, while still not clear-cut, had been significantly clarified. And after 13 years as editor in chief, I had the ability to effect change in the area for which I had been held accountable—marketing.

Throughout the 1990s I continued to wrestle with the problem of declining circulation. The conundrum I faced was this: most subscribers wanted the *Review* every week, but most nonsubscribers, especially young adults, wanted it to come less frequently.

How to find a way out of this impasse? I thought and thought, and came up with an idea. It was a major departure. I drew up a paper, and without showing it to anyone else, sent it e-mail to my boss, Elder Folkenberg. This was in January 1995.

I don't know where the elder was when he accessed my proposal, but from the depths of cyberspace the answer came back: "Go for it!" He became the first and most ardent advocate for the reinvention of the *Review*.

The essence of the new plan was *reader choices*. Since some Adventists wanted the *Review* every week but others less frequently, we'd give them choices—they could subscribe for three issues (they already received the NAD edition), two issues, or one issue each month. And each issue through the month would have its own identity, so that a reader could pick up a copy and not find themselves in the middle of a series of articles.

Robert Folkenberg immediately bought into the plan, but the *Review* editors took longer—much longer. We spent many hours discussing and arguing. Eventually we agreed that one of the three issues should have a world, mission focus; one a focus on youth and young adults; and the remaining one a focus on doctrine and heritage (these issues became tagged as the World Edition, Cutting Edge, and AnchorPoints).

It was the plan to shape an issue for the younger generation of Adventists that divided the editors. Not over the need for it—all were agreed that we had to try to bring younger subscribers on board—but whether the church leaders would permit us to make this issue, in content and appearance, as different as we felt it needed to be to appeal to the intended audience. Would we expend many hours of creative activity only to have our efforts squashed when the new issue hit the fan?

The whole new plan called for a lot of work—it entailed, in effect, the creation of three new *Reviews*—but Cutting Edge was the most problematic. We went back and forth, meeting after meeting, the editors divided. I felt anxious, uncertain how to bring the staff together. When I was near the end of my rope during one meeting, Roy Adams quietly spoke up. "Friends," he said, "we have no choice. Either we take a chance and go forward, or the *Review* will die on our watch."

His words summed it all up. Those opposing the plan dropped their objections. We would go forward.

Thus, 10 years after the "new *Review*" of 1986, another "new *Review*" rolled off the presses. It came larger, with color, and a graceful new design. It came as one magazine but with four faces: NAD, World Edition, Cutting Edge, and AnchorPoints. And it was launched by a Sabbath afternoon concert in the General Conference auditorium, hosted by the singing group Faith First and carried live by satellite.

The concert was a hit, especially as the first copies of the reinvented *Review* were distributed to the audience. It looked beautiful. It was indeed an exciting new product. We had invested a huge amount of time and effort into the new creation, and the General Conference Treasury had advanced funds, as had the Review and Herald, to make it happen.

I felt overwhelmed. Less than 15 months earlier I had sent the fateful e-mail to Pastor Folkenberg. Now, in April 1996, the dream had become reality.

Despite the widespread acclaim for the new *Review*, Adventists did not flock to subscribe. The numbers turned up, but not sharply. With marketing now coming under my new responsibilities as executive publisher, we contracted with Mind Over Media, a consulting firm recently established by Ray Tetz. Mind Over Media planned the launch concert, then embarked on a direct-mail campaign. *Surely,* we all thought, *if Adventists can only see the new* Review, *they will want to buy it.*

We were wrong. The direct-mail returns ran only a little better than industry averages, and only about 2 percent of Adventists subscribed from this approach. We were all surprised and disappointed.

The most radical aspect of the initial plan—the choice of subscribing to one, two, or three issues each month—was never implemented. Those involved in implementing the marketing, in consultation with the Review and Herald, decided that the idea would be too complicated to introduce along with the other changes. For its part, the publishing house was concerned that the plan might threaten its established subscriber base, as readers chose to change from receiving the church paper every week to every other week or just once per month.

Ever since, I have wondered: *What if?* The idea of choices was sound in theory—it addressed the conundrum I wrestled with over frequency of the *Review*. But would it have worked? It seemed too difficult to try to implement then. Would it seem too difficult today?

Circulation figures rose, but it soon became obvious that the goal of 100,000 was more elusive than ever. But all the effort and money was not for naught. The new *Review* launched in 1996 breathed new life and creativity into the church paper, ensuring its future for at least another 10 years.

For several years news editor Carlos Medley had tried to convince me and other members of the *Adventist Review* team that we should put the paper online. We dragged our feet. Getting the *Review* to press every week kept us plenty busy. Besides, how would we fund an online edition? The General Conference already had set up its own Web site, and it was not about to pay for the operation of another.

But Carlos didn't give up. He kept pressing, and slowly built up a cadre of donors for the proposed project. At last I took his proposal to the Publishing Board. They listened, assented, and told us to go ahead—on our own funding.

So the *Adventist Review* Web site came into being on September 30, 1999. The Treasury helped us with some start-up money, but ever since, the site has been self-funded. It has grown from strength to strength: more than 60,000 visitors from 148 countries and territories, who log in more than 220,000 times each month. Throughout the period, every year save one, the Web site has operated in the black. It currently has a healthy balance in reserves.

More than any other aspect of the *Review* office, the *Adventist Review* Web site has been associated with a single person. Carlos Medley dreamed it. Carlos Medley raised the funding. And Carlos Medley supervises it, changing the copy frequently and innovating with new features. Carlos Medley worked day and night—literally. For much of the time he added the Web site operation to his full-time responsibilities as news editor.

The years since 1999 have revealed Carlos' prescience in urging us as a staff to go online. Today, all print publications—even the best-known newspapers, such as the New York *Times* and the Washington *Times*, and magazines like *Time* and *Newsweek*—face an ongoing struggle to survive. All have established online editions, to which readers and advertisers gravitate in ever-increasing numbers.

———————

One morning, as I sat at breakfast in the cafeteria of Atlantic Union College, where I was visiting for camp meeting speaking engagements, a woman and small child approached me. I did not know her, but she had an idea she wished to present to me.

She said that she loved the *Review,* especially its reports and stories about the world church and mission, but wished we could find a way to bring its message to kids like her own child. "If you started an *Adventist Review* for kids," she argued, "you could get parents to subscribe and also build up reader loyalty. When the kids grow up, they will want to subscribe."

Great idea! Such magazines as *National Geographic,* along with newspapers such as the Washington *Post,* already prepared special kids' editions or sections. How could we do something similar for the *Adventist Review?*

I presented her idea to the editors. They liked it, but two obstacles stood in the way: staff and money. Everyone already was on full throttle, and the General Conference Treasury made no provision for ongoing funding for new projects.

The idea lapsed.

The woman wrote, reminding us. We discussed possibilities, but still couldn't see a way around the problems. But the idea was never far from our minds.

Then a couple of people heard about the idea and sent some start-up money. We talked more and prayed and decided to go ahead in faith. If the Lord wanted a kids' paper to happen, He would open the way.

So another segment was added to the office's growing circle of ministries. *KidsView* appeared in August 2002. Just four pages long, it was wholly prepared in the *Adventist Review* office and inserted into the *Review* once a month. Staff members Bonita Shields, Kim Maran, and Merle Poirier simply added the additional work to their load. We sold ads to bring in funding; we scratched and clawed to keep the new endeavor afloat. At times I wondered if it would survive.

Now as I write, *KidsView* is alive and well. It has expanded to eight pages and reaches in Adventist elementary schools around North America. The seed planted in a New England cafeteria has sprouted and bloomed. The Lord has put His stamp of blessing on it.

I am a person who looks forward rather than backward. I spend little time going over the past, so preparing this chapter has been an eye-opener. The events and initiatives I have penned here—and others might have been included—leave me with a sense of amazement and gratitude for which I can only give thanks to my gracious Christ, the Lord of the work.

With all the effort, the struggles, the hopes, the disappointments, the Lord was always there. All praise belongs to Him for His energizing and sustaining power in the multiple reinventing of the *Adventist Review*.

What I did not know in 1986, or 1991, or 1996, or 1999, or 2000—what I did not even dream of—was that the most sweeping change would still lie ahead.

CHAPTER 15

Embracing the Impossible

See, I am doing a new thing!
Now it springs up; do you not perceive it?
—Isaiah 43:19

As I approached three score and 10, I began to consider retiring from the *Adventist Review* office. I still enjoyed the work, but I didn't want questions about the editor's age to occupy people's minds rather than the *Review* itself. I wanted to leave while I was still appreciated.

Every time I broached the topic with my boss, Pastor Paulsen, he urged me to carry on. Eventually, however, we agreed that I would see the paper through the General Conference session in 2005, to be held in St. Louis, Missouri, and then hand over the reins to another.

For some time the Review and Herald and I had agreed on my writing another book of daily devotional readings. The earlier one, *Behold His Glory*, released in 1989, had been well received, but I knew how much work writing a page a day for a year entailed. We set a series of dates for me to submit the book manuscript, but each time I backed off because of the pressures of work. At last, in early February 2004, we settled on a definite time frame, and I committed to providing the finished manuscript to the publishing house by the close of 2005.

I was still able to work hard and cover a lot of ground, but I found myself feeling more tired than usual at the close of a long day. With the preparations for the daily session *Bulletins,* my life would be quite full with handling the book manuscript in my spare time, but I felt up to it. It would be a strong close to my tenure at the *Review,* working at capacity until I left office after the General Conference session.

Within days of making the commitment to the Review and Herald, a startling new development, utterly unexpected and unforeseen, took over my life.

———•◆•———

February 18, 2004: The date was marked on my office calendar. I had made an appointment to discuss with Pastor Paulsen a problem that was causing me concern.

He quickly brushed aside the matter, telling me to forget about it. Then he fixed me with his eye. "Bill," he said, "I have something I want to talk to you about."

He appreciated the content of the *Adventist Review*, he said, but it needed to circulate in far greater numbers. With world church membership now more than 12 million and growing rapidly overseas, the General Conference needed a common vehicle to help keep Adventists united. So here was the assignment: Get the *Adventist Review* staff together and figure out a way to send the church paper—without charge—to at least 500,000 homes each month, and preferably 1 million. Study the areas of the world in which English is used and focus on them. Later, if funds become available, the plan can be extended to other languages. Our job at the *Review* office: Work out how to do it—how to produce the *Review* for the world church, how to distribute it, and how much it would cost.

Pastor Paulsen made two aspects crystal clear. We could not expect additional help in the assignment, and when we had put together a plan, he could offer no assurance that the funding for it would be available.

It was a breathtaking assignment, comprehensive, global in its dimensions. But in concept not entirely new. Over the years the need for literature for the world church had frequently been voiced, but no one had ever followed up. Now the General Conference president was taking the initiative to make something happen on an ongoing basis.

I called my staff together and laid out Pastor Paulsen's challenge. They rose to the occasion with scarcely a demurral. It would be the first of many, many conferences as we gave ourselves to the task. Throughout the next many months the staff, knowing full well that all their efforts might be for naught, poured themselves into the exciting new project.

Very soon six dimensions of the assignment became apparent:

1. **Editorial.** What content should the publication have? What relation should it bear to the *Review*? What should it be called?
2. **Design.** How should it be designed to appeal to Adventists of vastly different backgrounds?
3. **Production**. How to prepare and print one magazine on a global scale?
4. **Distribution.** How to get the magazine to Adventists in places as varied as the villages of Africa, homes in the Caribbean, and church members in the islands of the Pacific, in Asia, and Europe?
5. **Finances.** What would the total scheme cost per year, and where could funding for it be obtained?
6. **Impact on the weekly *Review*.** With membership in North America already receiving the NAD edition without charge, and now the new paper available to them once a month through their local church, would they still want to subscribe to the weekly *Review*?

Organizing the staff into task forces to focus on each of these areas, we went to work. In the first two areas—content and design— we were on familiar ground, but for the challenges of production and distribution there was no model in the church or outside the church to which we might look for guidance. We would have to rely on the Lord to show us the way.

The Lord provided key people to enable the project to succeed. With so many individuals pitching in, I hesitate to single out anyone. Nevertheless, the story would be incomplete without mention of the large contributions of several men and women.

Steve Rose, undertreasurer of the General Conference, played a vital role. His job description made him responsible for the General Conference budget and therefore directly involved in the funding dimension of the project. But he did far more than oversee finances. He believed in the idea and did all in his power to make it a reality. He and I worked closely together, discussing possibilities and finding a way through problems.

Planning called for a mass of data gathering. We needed to explore printing possibilities in many countries, had to get information on shipping routes, times and costs, and so on. The size and complexity of what was contemplated threatened to overwhelm me. One day, almost thinking out loud, I shared with the staff my desperate need of someone to assist me in getting all the information we would need to have in order to make critical decisions. After a few hours Merle Poirier approached me and volunteered to help. By her choice Merle worked only part-time, but she was thorough and well organized. She had the ability to see the big picture while being careful of details. She turned out to be just the right person for what was needed. Before the year was up, she would work long hours and even holidays, gathering, assembling, and analyzing a mass of data.

As the outline of the project began to materialize, with the Korean Publishing House playing an important part, we realized the need to have someone on the ground who could work out and oversee distribution of the paper for Asia. Pastor P. D. Chun had retired from the presidency of the Northern Asia-Pacific Division, but he graciously consented to take up work on a part-time basis. His counsel, understanding of the field, and service proved invaluable.

Jeff Dever, a top-level Adventist designer in the Washington, D.C., area, became the one responsible for the look of the new magazine. He put together a design that would "work" in Europe as well as in North America, in Africa as well as Asia; and one that would be flexible enough to accommodate translation if and when the church was ready to take that step. As the deadline for the first issue drew near, we ran into a crisis situation, and Jeff and his staff saved the day for us.

We had much to learn about production, printing, and shipping possibilities and little time to catch up. Again, someone was there to help us. Ed Boyle, an Adventist layperson who works in the printing industry, furnished timely information and suggestions.

The Good Book says, "Before they call I will answer" (Isa. 65:24). That was exactly what happened to turn the dream of a global magazine into reality.

After several months the contours of the new magazine began to emerge.

It would be a 32-page monthly, with full color throughout. Articles would be one or two pages long, except for the cover story, which would be four pages. The cover story would always appear in the center and highlight an aspect of the church's mission. The paper would not run advertising; and every aspect of it would be planned to unite Adventists everywhere in one hope, one identity, one mission, and one lifestyle. Each issue would feature an article on one of our fundamental beliefs, as well as a clip-out Bible study in basic English that could be used in literacy classes. An article on Ellen White or our SDA heritage would run each time, as would a page on world health and another focusing on a particular country, with its mission challenge. And every issue of the magazine would provide space for the General Conference president to share a pastoral or leadership message.

In conjunction with General Conference leadership, we toyed with several names for this special issue: *Adventist Review*, World Edition; *Adventist Review*, Global Edition; and so on. Eventually, because the magazine would have its own character, we settled on *Adventist World*. We wanted it to be international in all aspects. I urged the staff to find writers and articles from the world of Adventism, and to weed out all American expressions and illustrations.

From the mass of data relative to production, printing, and shipping we reached the conclusion that the magazine should be printed and distributed to cover four zones—North America, Central America, and Western Europe; Africa; Asia; and the South Pacific. By sending it bulk, we could print 1 million copies each month, at a total cost of just a little more than $2 million annually. We based our calculations on 5 members accessing each copy. Thus the proposed magazine would reach five or more million Adventist each month—a significant proportion of the world church.

We were able to put together a document for leaders of the world church to consider when they gathered in October for the 2004 Annual Council. The working proposal generated a great deal of interest, with many expressions of support. Only one significant objection was raised: the plan covered only Adventists who could read English. But it would be a step—and a big one. The council voted strongly for the proposal to move ahead.

———————

With the approval for the overall plan, we now had to wrestle with specifics—and that meant figuring out the best way to meet the need in Africa. I badly wanted a printing site located in Africa, and we invited bids from several printers—church-owned and otherwise—on that continent. At the same time we looked at costs and shipping expenses and delivery times from printing bases in England, Germany, Denmark, Portugal, India, United Arab Emirates, and Korea.

Then we faced a critical decision. The numbers showed that the most economical site would be one located in North America. Printing costs in Africa were simply prohibitive. Reluctantly I gave up that hope.

So the four zones of the world church would be serviced this way: North and Central America plus Western Europe, from North America; Africa, also from North America; Asia, from Korea; and the South Pacific, from Australia. This configuration in turn suggested the involvement of three Adventist publishing houses: the Review and Herald in the United States, the Korean Publishing House in Seoul, and the Signs Publishing Company near Melbourne.

The plan was beginning to take on flesh and bones, but one huge issue remained unsolved: How would it be funded?

Undertreasurer Steve Rose had a hope, a wish, a dream. He knew that in banks in Korea, the General Conference had money given by members that had been accumulating for years. Because of government regulations that imposed a heavy tax on withdrawing these funds as hard currency, the General Conference had not been able to utilize them. Could a way be found to tap these funds for financing the new project?

There was no government restriction on withdrawing these moneys in won, the local currency. But what printer would be willing to accept payment in won?

At least one, we discovered. Lane Press, a high-class company located in Burlington, Vermont and specializing in magazine printing, studied possibilities and told us they would accept payment in won. Already we had noticed the company because of its competitive rates and know-how concerning shipping to Africa. It seemed to us to be the site to look to for handling the needs of Africa.

So we proposed that the Review and Herald handle North and Central America plus Western Europe; Lane Press print for Africa;

the Korean Publishing House for Asia; and Signs Publishing Company for the South Pacific. Funding for the second and third zones would come from Korean won while the South Pacific Division already had agreed to cover most of the costs of zone 4. Funds would have to be found for the first zone, but the other areas of the world were now cared for.

In the spring of 2005 we presented the printing plan to the Administrative Committee. It resulted in lively discussion, which extended through two sessions of the committee. Members were divided over the involvement of Lane Press, a non-Adventist company. Some argued that the Review and Herald, which under the plan already had the lion's share of the work, should also print for Africa. After the second session of debate, the chair called for a vote by secret ballot. The plan as recommended carried by a strong margin.

———•◆•———

Although we had made strides in putting together a funding plan, there was still a big gap—the $1 million or so needed to fund North and Inter-America, and Western Europe. The General Conference no longer has a "deep pocket." It carries only a contingency fund. By now Pastor Paulsen had decided that the new magazine should be given priority—it would go forward in spite of the financial difficulties. That meant that Steve Rose would have to adjust the General Conference budget to make room for it.

Steve, along with the General Conference legal office, had tried hard to find a way to access the church's funds locked up in Korea. In spring 2005 I joined him as he made another trip to Seoul and we met with a Mr. Baik, a leading tax attorney at the largest law firm in the country. As we met in his large, comfortable office, we hoped to receive a good word from him. Instead, he walked us through the government regulations concerning the transfer of hard currency in relation to the proposed magazine—and the news was bad. The only way we could access the funds in dollars would be for the new paper to be based in Korea, with a Korean editor and publisher. He saw no way to get past the legal stipulations.

It was a disappointment, and we returned to the United States feeling deflated. Then Pastor P. D. Chun, who had been with us when we met with Mr. Baik, asked for permission to try a different tack. Through his longtime leadership of the church in Korea, he knew people who knew people who knew . . . Eventually he was able to make contact with a leading government individual. They went out to dine, and at the end of a pleasant meal the government official asked, "Now, how can I help you?"

"Well, sir, we have this problem . . ."

"Let me see, let me see what I can do."

After a short time Pastor Chun sent us a message that seemed too good to be true. The Bank of Korea would permit disbursement in hard currency for the expenses of the project outside Korea! It seemed a miraculous breakthrough.

How had a way been found? Yes, the regulations were clear and unbending, but they also provided for exceptions to be granted.

To all of us involved in the new magazine, this opening up of funds was perhaps the clearest and most dramatic in a series of incidents that revealed the Lord's guiding hand over the project. And it was all done without any bending of the law or money under the table. Even the meal came free—the government official insisted on paying the bill!

The months leading up to the release of *Adventist World* became a blur. My colleagues and I continually faced new issues, some major, some minor. We had to make rapid decisions, for time was running out. Many times I left work with a problem that needed to be resolved. Many times I rose at 3:00 a.m. to wrestle with it. By the time I walked into the office at 8:00 I had the answer.

It was an amazing, exciting, exhausting time.

One big issue remained: distribution in North America. The

funding plan was based on bulk distribution through the churches—direct mailing to the home would be prohibitive. But church leaders, at both division and union levels, doubted that the plan would work for North America. They feared that copies of *Adventist World* would pile up in local churches, unread and devalued.

And the issue of the impact of the new journal on the circulation of the weekly *Review* was still there, unresolved, as it had been since we began work on the project.

Then Elder Don Schneider broke through the impasse. He had discussed possibilities with his colleagues, and they had an idea. How about dropping the NAD edition and replacing it with the *Adventist World*? If we would permit the division to have eight pages dedicated in each issue to specific concerns of their field, the change from the NAD edition to the *Adventist World* could be accomplished with minimum impact on production and finances.

Once again—just the solution we needed! Once again—the Lord going on ahead of us, opening the way!

———◆———

All this was happening while we were gearing up for the General Conference session. These five-yearly events tax the staffs of both the publishing house and *Adventist Review* office, as the church paper goes to press every night with news of the day. It's possible only by planning and preparing a lot of the copy months ahead.

And in my "spare" time I was struggling to complete the devotional book manuscript to which I had committed just before the *Adventist World* assignment came to us.

That year, 2005, was the most hectic of my life. I have always worked hard and productively, but 2005 saw a breaking out beyond all previous efforts. It was exhilarating—the handling of multiple decisions, the problem solving—but it was also dangerous. I knew that I was pushing myself perilously close to the edge.

The General Conference session left all of us exhausted, but there could be no letup. Now we were racing to prepare for the first issue of the *Adventist World* for electronic transmission to the four printing suites. And then we ran into a crisis.

The Review and Herald team had done outstanding work in getting out the daily *Bulletins* of the General Conference session. Now, immediately after the around-the-clock effort demanded by that task, they were faced with producing a brand-new product, a start-up magazine. Its design, graceful but intricate in details, gave them headaches.

Time was running out, and I was worried. Presses around the world had been given a schedule, and it looked as though we would not meet it.

Each July our family plans a week at the beach. This year our children and grandchildren had come from abroad for this time together—the highlight of the Johnssons' year. But July 2005 brought no joy by the sea for me. I spent untold hours on the telephone—sometimes a whole morning—trying to keep the first issue on schedule. The family tried to understand, but I was a big disappointment to them, especially to my grandkids.

As the days passed, I became convinced that publishing house personnel, overburdened with many other demands on their time and energy, could not prepare the new magazine in time to meet the production deadline. In desperation I called Jeff Dever, who understood the new design—he had created it! He and his team took it over. We met the schedule.

When I held the first issue of the *Adventist World* in my hands, I scarcely could keep back tears. The ideas we had poured into it and the design features that we had worked through with Jeff Dever now had flesh and bones. They had materialized.

And it was all very good, *so* good.

My heart welled up to the Lord in gratitude.

The *Adventist World*, something I had never even dreamed of, was the biggest undertaking of my life. It brought me incredible satisfaction and fulfillment.

And also pain. For during a board meeting of the Review and Herald Publishing Association Steve Rose and I came under severe criticism for our role in the planning that brought Lane Press into the circle. Speech after speech castigated us for disloyalty to the publishing house. It was the sharpest rebuke I had endured in nearly 50 years of ministry.

In vain Steve and I pointed out that the decision to involve Lane Press was made by the General Conference Administrative Committee, with a strong majority voting for it and the president in the chair. In vain I reminded them of my statement to the same board 10 years earlier about a possible conflict of interest. They would not be convinced. Caught off guard—the matter was not listed on the agenda for the day—I forgot a critical component of the plan that the Administrative Committee voted: that before the permission had come for release of hard currency funds, Lane was prepared to be paid in won. Sharing that information might have made a difference.

I do not fault those many who beat up on Steve and me that day. They spoke in the interests of the Review and Herald, which they should have done as members of its board. Steve and I also loved the house and supported it, but we had been charged with guiding a project that involved the world church. We strove hard to ensure that the new magazine would keep within budget, in the long term as well as short.

The *Adventist World* still gives me much satisfaction. Now in its third year as I write this, it still looks and reads well. Not one aspect has been adjusted—not a detail of design or content. That, I think, is remarkable in a completely new magazine.

———◆———

My mind goes back over the years to the way my *Review* journey began. I think of the heady optimism and determination to
break the 100,000 circulation barrier. I think of the ideas, the
striving, the plans, the efforts, the travels—and of my slow, sad re-
alization that the 100,000 mark was unattainable.

With pressures from the Internet and competing publications,
more and more the struggle became one of bare survival, holding
on to what we had.

And then—surprise!

I held in my hand the first issue of the *Adventist World*. Printed on
presses in four different locations, it had a run of 1.1 million copies.

I had dreamed in terms of 100,000.

The Lord, who is able to do far, far more than we can plan or
even imagine, the Lord of abundant measure, measure pressed
down and running over, the God of the impossible, gave more
than tenfold.

Home Again

CHAPTER 16

And the Story Goes On

But he said to me, "My grace is sufficient for you,
for my power is made perfect in weakness."
—Paul, 2 Corinthians 12:9

I began retirement on January 1, 2007. It lasted all of 17 days. Three Adventist universities—Loma Linda, La Sierra, and Southern—had invited me to teach for them. I was attracted to Loma Linda, not only because of the high regard I have for the institution and its staff, but for the opportunity of sharing insights from the Word in a medical setting. Discussions reached the stage of working out schedules and classes.

Then my old boss, Pastor Paulsen, made an offer. Would I work part-time as his assistant for interfaith relations? Would I spearhead dialogues with other Christian churches, but also develop contacts with leaders of the world religions—beginning with Islam? The time had come, the elder stated, for our growing church to take new initiatives. I didn't labor over a decision. The new assignment seemed just right for me. For some 20 years I had been involved as a member of the Adventist team in conversations with other churches; I felt I still had plenty to contribute to the work of the church.

It has proved to be all that I envisioned. I work out of a home office, at my own pace. There is travel, including some abroad, but far less than I had while *Review* editor. And the Muslim initiative has stretched my mind: new reading, new planning, new people. I started entirely from scratch. And, as always in the past, the Lord has led down paths untrod. We have made an excellent start on building bridges. As with everything connected with the church, mission is foremost. Our goal is to help leaders of Islam at the highest levels become acquainted with Seventh-day Adventists, helping them to realize that we are not just another Christian group but a body separate and distinct, with beliefs and practices that resonate with Islam.

As I approached retirement, some friends and family were concerned as to how I would handle the change. After getting up early every morning to be first at the office, after carrying the burden of the weekly issues for 24 years—what would happen when all that was stripped away?

Let me tell you: Not for one day have I missed the office. The people, yes, but not the office. I enjoyed the work, but that is behind me.

Been there, done that.

Time to move on.

Thank God for new days, new challenges.

The last months at the *Review* drained me to the last drop. After the amazing, frenetic year 2005 with the General Conference session, launch of *Adventist World*, and completion of the manuscript for *Jesus: A Heart Full of Grace*, I hoped to coast to the finish line in 2006.

It was not to be. The appointment of a successor took much longer than expected. As the year dragged on, I struggled toward the light at the end of the tunnel. I was out of gas. I was losing weight. I wondered which would come first—the exit or a breakdown in health.

Somehow the good Lord, the Lord of grace all-sufficient, brought me through.

Noelene retired six months ahead of me. At the end of the year together we were feted and farewelled on occasion after occasion until it seemed almost too much. "Any more of these speeches and we'll start to believe it and get swelled heads," we told the well-wishers.

I also stated that from here on family would come first. Where I went, Noelene would go too. Our children, Terry and Julie, would have priority, along with our granddaughters Madeleine and Jacqueline. After that, the larger family—Noelene's brothers, Barry and Bernard, at Loma Linda, plus relatives in Australia. We planned to travel plenty, no longer at the fevered pace of the past many years, but just to enjoy the company of dear ones.

Early in 2007 we bought the plane tickets. At the end of January we'd go to Loma Linda. In February we'd visit our daughter in Chicago. March—a long trip to our son and his family in Dubai. Finally, in April a visit to Oz, where a big family reunion was planned.

Plans in place. Tickets in hand. All set to go. Sunday morning we leave for California.

And then Friday morning, a telephone call . . .

———◆◆———

On the line was Dr. Gravino, a cardiologist. Noelene, who had been experiencing slight pain in the neck when we went walking, had been to his office the day before for a nuclear stress test.

He said, "I strongly advise you to postpone your trip to California. You should have an angiogram without delay."

Noelene tried to argue, said she could get the angiogram at Loma Linda. But after she and I talked a bit, she called him back and told him we had decided to reschedule the California visit.

So the next week found her in Washington Adventist Hospital for an angiogram. She and I did not expect any major problem to surface—she had taken care of her diet and walked regularly. One stent, two stents—this would be the worst treatment she would need. But when Dr. Gravino called me out of the waiting room, he told me, "Your wife needs immediate surgery. Four arteries have blockages; and one is 95 percent blocked."

Gravino had another doctor with him. He introduced him as

231

Dr. Militano, a surgeon, whom he was recommending for the procedure. He, in turn, explained the risks and stressed that there was no time for delay. The only question was whether Noelene should be taken immediately to surgery, or whether they would wait until the next morning.

It was all so sudden. It was almost too much. But with the shock came a sense of deep gratitude. If Noelene had gotten on that plane to California three days before, she might not have reached Loma Linda alive.

That evening before the surgery, Noelene was calm and peaceful. She joked with the friends and staff who came by. When a woman chaplain asked her if she was afraid of the pain, she replied, "No, I'm not afraid of it."

"You're not? How come?"

"Listen, I've had two children!"

I left her about 10:00 p.m. and tried to get some sleep. At 2:00 a.m. I was wide awake, shivering with cold and fear. I thought of the saw slicing through her chest bone, her chest flayed open, her body violated—that body that had been my companion, that had borne our children, that I loved—and my blood turned to ice.

I was in hell, a frozen hell.

I reached out to words that have sustained me over the years. I repeated to myself my favorite texts: "My grace is sufficient for you, for my power is made perfect in weakness" (2 Cor. 12:9). And the ancient words of Moses: "The eternal God is your refuge, and underneath are the everlasting arms" (Deut. 33:27). I clung to God's promises, clung by my fingernails.

The psalmist wrote: "If I make my bed in hell, behold, You are there" (Ps. 139:8, NKJV).

It's true, I made my bed in hell. But God was there.

I got up, read the Bible, prayed, put on a favorite CD of T. Marshall Kelly's music. "Never doubt God's love for you . . ." His words seeped into my soul. I sat back in the easy chair. The CD ran its full course. I started it over. I clung to the words of Paul and Moses.

About 4:00 a.m. I bundled up and went walking for an hour. I walked, thinking and talking with the Lord. Then I returned home, showered, and drove to the hospital.

It was only 6:00, but everyone was astir. Noelene had slept well. We spent a precious, tearful last 20 minutes together. "If I don't make it," she said, "tell Terry and Julie that I love them, and that I'll see them in the morning."

Then onto the gurney, down the elevator, and into the surgery block. I stayed with her till they wheeled her away and the doors closed.

The waiting room was deserted. I found a big easy chair and tried to rest. Suddenly a hand touched my shoulder. It was Bob Nixon, who had come to be with me. "Let's go and get breakfast," he said, taking my arm.

Throughout the morning a steady stream of friends and staff came by to pray and show support. And then it was Julie, who had come straight from the airport, where she had flown in from Chicago.

The hours ticked slowly away. Just after noon Dr. Militano appeared. "Everything went fine," he said. "Your wife now has the arteries of a 35-year-old." He explained that he had performed the triple bypass surgery by the "off pump" method, which avoided the use of the heart machine and reduced the risk factors.

By the next day Noelene was out of intensive care and dropping zingers. To a friend who remarked on Julie's presence: "See what lengths I'll go to have my daughter visit me?"

Two days later, just 72 hours after the surgery, she came home, entrusted to my care. Now I became nurse, cook, and bottle washer, waiting on her around the clock, day and night, not leaving the house unless someone else took my place.

She had waited on me for 47 years; now it was my turn. And it was a privilege. The hardest part was lack of sleep—all night I dozed half awake, alert to any sound from her.

During that week and those that followed we spent almost all our time together. It had been a long, long time since that had happened—only way back in the first months after our marriage when we sailed to India and went into language school. Just having her there, seeing her strength return, sitting down to eat together, to watch a DVD—it was a precious time we would not trade for anything.

Yes, our travel plans went out the window, but the Lord spared her life. The California trip—gone. Chicago—gone. Dubai—gone. The Oz trip—not gone. A few days before we were to leave at the end of March, Dr. Gravino cleared her to fly. When the Johnsson clan gathered down under, against all expectations we were there.

Noelene's emergency surgery—that was the first whammy. The second followed close behind.

For years I have had an annual physical examination, and year by year the tests came back negative. "It's all a waste of time and money," I joked. "They never find anything wrong with me."

In December 2006, just as I was about to leave the *Review*, something showed up: I was anemic. Iron pills soon brought the hemoglobin level back to normal, but my physician was concerned. What was going on?

He ordered a series of tests, and eventually an endoscopy. With this the patient is anesthetized and a small light and camera lowered through the mouth into the stomach. The physician sees all on a TV monitor. Because of the sedation, you aren't permitted to drive yourself home after the test.

On Valentine's Day Bob Nixon drove me out to Gaithersburg for the test. It was a snowy, blustery day; the streets were empty, with vehicles abandoned along the way. At the medical facility few patients had showed up, and I was taken in immediately for the procedure.

When I woke up, the first words I heard from the physician were

"You have a malignancy of the stomach." He showed me photographs from my stomach. A mass of nodules was clearly visible. Some had tiny red circles around them—where my blood was seeping out.

The physician went on. There was a 95 percent likelihood that the cancer was a carcinoma, in which case the only treatment was surgery, followed by a long recuperation. The other possibility was lymphoma, which could be treated without surgery, but that was only a small likelihood.

I was still dopey from the anesthesia and barely grasped the import of his words. My friend, Bob, however, heard it all and was badly shaken by the prospect. He tried to stay upbeat, but slowly the reality of what lay ahead began to impact me.

For a couple days I struggled to come to terms with the fact: I had cancer. Impossible! I ran marathons; I didn't get cancer. I felt too well. My blood pressure was 120/70, my resting heart rate 45. Me, with cancer? Not possible!

For a short while, 15 or 20 minutes, I lapsed into self-pity, but quickly snapped out of it. I would face this thing. I would embrace it. Nor could I feel angry with God. He had given me 72 good years, and if the days ahead were to be dark and uncertain, so be it. He would be there for me, come what may.

The most difficult aspect of these days following the sudden intrusion of the C word was relating to others. News like this is a very private thing, and before you face the world you need to work through your future privately, by yourself. Unfortunately, word of the prognosis leaked out before I had fully processed matters. I found it very difficult at church, a few days later, when well-meaning saints came up to me and said, with knowing looks, "You are in my prayers."

It nagged at me. The prospect of dealing with a carcinoma was pretty grim, but the biopsy reports were not yet in. What if it wasn't a carcinoma after all? In imagination I visualized friends and acquaintances writing off my future, and I rebelled at the thought. I wasn't finished. I would fight this thing.

After tossing in bed all night with this nagging thought, I decided to take an initiative. I would write something deliberately lighthearted that would let the world know that I planned to be around for a long while. I got up and went to the computer. Singling out Roy Adams and Kimberly Maran for specific mention because they would appreciate a joke, I sent the following e-mail to Rachel Child, my super assistant when I was editor:

"Dear Friends,

"Thank you for the kind messages and prayers. And for replenishing my chocolate supply, which was running low. I detect Rachel's hand in this.

"OK, I have decided to share the medical news with you. If you find these sorts of things too gross or too technical to stomach (Kim and Roy, take note), skip to the bottom line. On Valentine's Day a doctor who probably should have, like you, taken the day off, went on a fishing expedition—inside me. He dropped a line with a light and a camera down my gullet (should that be gizzard?—unsure of the scientific term here). A TV monitor recorded the action, but I found the movie boring and slept right through it.

"In the ocean depths the doc encountered a slow-moving object—a chocolate éclair! No, just kidding. It was some sort of formation he is still trying to figure out. Noelene thinks it will turn out to have a curry base, but my money is on chocolate.

"Experiences like these make you really think. I am now ready to preach on Jeremiah 4:19, where the prophet cries out, "My guts! My guts!" (A translation definitely preferred over the KJV, which will send modern audiences to the exits posthaste. Check it out.)

"So how am I really feeling? Great, and I'm not kidding. I have high energy, physically and mentally, and with Noelene now cleared to start driving again, I am itching to get back to the good stuff. There are books to write, dialogues with Islam to launch, marathons to run. Looks like I may have to settle for a further delay, but it will be no more than a hiatus.

"There you have it. I hope Kim and Roy got to the end without throwing up.

"Love you all.

"Bill.

"PS: Peter Landless came by, also bearing chocolate. My cup runneth over. And to think that Noelene, with the zeal of a woman with a new heart, has sworn off chocolate! Gluttony, get behind me!"

◆

Sabbath morning I put on boots and heavy coat and went tramping through the snow in the lovely park near our home. A cardinal gleamed startling red in the white world. I wondered if I would be here one year longer to see another cardinal. Would I be around for my favorite time of the year, the greening of the trees in April?

As I walked and talked to the Lord and myself, a plan of attack began to crystallize. I would fight this thing with all my might, following what I called an FEL strategy: faith, exercise, and laughter. Come what may, I would trust God. I would keep walking, walking until I couldn't walk anymore, until the bad guys in my tummy said, "Let's get out of here and find some place more comfortable!" And I would shame away the cancer by scorning it. No more evening news, no more downbeat books or movies, only happy endings.

The following day I shared the FEL plan of attack with Dr. Peter Landless, a wonderful physician friend. "Add another L!" he exclaimed. "Make it FELL—faith, exercise, laughter, and Landless! I'll be there to see you through."

◆

Tuesday morning the telephone rang. The biopsy results had just come in. "I'm so sorry," said the doctor's assistant. "You have lymphoma."

I felt like shouting out, "Praise God! Hallelujah! I have lymphoma!"

The lab had analyzed the tumor to be a maltoma, a form of lymphoma that is treatable without surgery. It is associated with H. pilori, the bacterium that causes stomach ulcers. Years before I had twice gone through courses of antibiotics to remove this invader from my system, but the damage had been done.

Now I went through tests and more tests—CT scans, PET scans, bone marrow analysis—to determine if the cancer had spread beyond the stomach and how it should be attacked. After extensive consultations the chief oncologist who was caring for me settled on a course of radiation therapy—five times each day for four weeks.

I felt no pain from the radiation, but it took away my appetite. By the final week my stomach, irritated from the treatment, refused to admit even a glass of water. I could not stand the sight or smell of food and found it hard even to sit at my customary place at the table.

As my weight plunged, Noelene coaxed and cajoled me to eat. She resorted to stratagems, changing the location when she prepared a little Jell-O or broth. She poured loving concern into every ounce, every sip.

By the time the course of treatment was over and I had "graduated" with a certificate of completion, I was down to where Noelene and I started life together—139 pounds.

When people asked us, "How did you spend your first year in retirement?" we tell them, "In doctors' offices." Noelene worked with four physicians, I with a different four. It seemed we were forever going to an appointment or coming from one; forever facing another battery of tests. Altogether we spent at least three months of the year in health-related stuff.

But the year had far more for us. We went ahead with a camp meeting speaking appointment that we had agreed to before we retired. I was as frail as a quivering fern as I stood before the people, but the Lord came through with a remarkable blessing. We spent a wonderful month at the beach with family. We took a cruise along the east coast of America. I chaired dialogues with the World Evangelical Alliance, and the Presbyterian Church USA. And in November, my strength returning, I flew to Africa for two conferences. Then we left together for Dubai.

The year ended as it began, with a nuclear stress test for Noelene and an endoscopy for me. Dr. Gravino pronounced Noelene's heart in good shape, while the photographs from inside my tummy showed no trace of lymphoma.

It was a wonderful finale to one of the strangest but happiest years of our lives.

Time to close. Not to end—to close.

For the story goes on. It has no end. It is still being written.

It is still being written because grace has no end. God's love has no end.

The story goes on . . . and on. Into eternity the story goes on.

Eternity.

We were made for the stars.

Made to dream dreams, impossible dreams.

And to trust God to make them happen.

Why does George Knight say **this is the most important book** he's ever written?

The Apocalyptic VISION and the Neutering of ADVENTISM

Are we erasing our relevancy?

George R. Knight

Does the Adventist Church have any reason for existence if it has lost that which makes it different from all the rest of Christianity?

Why were the early Seventh-day Adventists so passionate about evangelizing the world?

How can we rekindle in our own lives that passion for spreading the gospel?

Could a revitalization of the apocalyptic vision provide the answer as the world and the church move toward the Second Coming?

Accept Knight's challenge to go back to your roots for the answers. (But beware—you may have to uproot yourself from the pew to be truly Adventist!) Paperback, 112 pages.